SOCIAL
ACTION

SOCIAL
ACTION

A Compilation Prepared by the
Research Department of the
Universal House of Justice

August 2020

BAHÁ'Í
PUBLISHING

WILMETTE, ILLINOIS

Bahá'í Publishing Trust
401 Greenleaf Avenue, Wilmette, Illinois 60091

Copyright © 2020 by the National Spiritual Assembly
of the Bahá'ís of the United States

23 22 21 20   4 3 2 1

ISBN 978-0-87743-414-6

Cover and book design by Patrick Falso

CONTENTS

UNDERLYING CONCEPTS AND PRINCIPLES

The Concept of Social and Economic Development Enshrined in the Teachings

Promote ye the development of the cities of God and His countries, and glorify Him therein in the joyous accents of His well-favored ones. In truth, the hearts of men are edified through the power of the tongue, even as houses and cities are built up by the hand and other means. We have assigned to every end a means for its accomplishment; avail yourselves thereof, and place your trust and confidence in God, the Omniscient, the All-Wise.

(Bahá'u'lláh, The Kitáb-i-Aqdas, ¶160)   [1]

. . . is not the object of every Revelation to effect a transformation in the whole character of mankind, a transformation that shall manifest itself, both outwardly and inwardly, that shall affect both its inner life and external conditions?

(Bahá'u'lláh, The Kitáb-i-Íqán, ¶270)   [2]

. . . that which hath streamed forth from the Most Exalted Pen is conducive to the glory, the advancement and education of all the peoples and kindreds of the earth. Indeed it is the sovereign remedy for every disease, could they but comprehend and perceive it.

(Bahá'u'lláh, *Tablets of Bahá'u'lláh Revealed after the Kitáb-i-Aqdas* (Wilmette: Bahá'í Publishing Trust, 1988), p. 73)   [3]

O people of God! Give ear unto that which, if heeded, will ensure the freedom, well-being, tranquility, exaltation and advancement of all men.

(Bahá'u'lláh, *Tablets of Bahá'u'lláh Revealed after the Kitáb-i-Aqdas,* p. 92)   [4]

Unveiled and unconcealed, this Wronged One hath, at all times, proclaimed before the face of all the peoples of the world that which will serve as the key for unlocking the doors of sciences, of arts, of knowledge, of well-being, of prosperity and wealth.

(Bahá'u'lláh, *Tablets of Bahá'u'lláh Revealed after the Kitáb-i-Aqdas,* p. 96)   [5]

The progress of the world, the development of nations, the tranquility of peoples, and the peace of all who dwell on earth are among the principles and ordinances of God. Religion bestoweth upon man the most precious of all gifts, offereth the cup of prosperity, imparteth eternal life, and showereth imperishable benefits upon mankind.

(Bahá'u'lláh, *Tablets of Bahá'u'lláh Revealed after the Kitáb-i-Aqdas,* pp. 129–130)   [6]

God, the True One, beareth Me witness, and every atom in existence is moved to testify that such means as lead to the elevation, the advancement, the education, the protection and the regeneration of the peoples of the earth have been clearly set forth by Us and are revealed in the Holy Books and Tablets by the Pen of Glory.

(Bahá'u'lláh, *Tablets of Bahá'u'lláh Revealed after the Kitáb-i-Aqdas,* p. 130)   [7]

That one indeed is a man who, today, dedicateth himself to the service of the entire human race. The Great Being saith: Blessed and happy is he that ariseth to promote the best interests of the peoples and kindreds of the earth.

(Bahá'u'lláh, *Tablets of Bahá'u'lláh Revealed after the Kitáb-i-Aqdas*, p. 167) [8]

This servant appealeth to every diligent and enterprising soul to exert his utmost endeavor and arise to rehabilitate the conditions in all regions and to quicken the dead with the living waters of wisdom and utterance, by virtue of the love he cherisheth for God, the One, the Peerless, the Almighty, the Beneficent.

(Bahá'u'lláh, *Tablets of Bahá'u'lláh Revealed after the Kitáb-i-Aqdas*, p. 172) [9]

Every age hath its own problem, and every soul its particular aspiration. The remedy the world needeth in its present-day afflictions can never be the same as that which a subsequent age may require. Be anxiously concerned with the needs of the age ye live in, and centre your deliberations on its exigencies and requirements.

(Bahá'u'lláh, *The Tabernacle of Unity: Bahá'u'lláh's Responses to Mánikchí Ṣáḥib and Other Writings* (Haifa: Bahá'í World Centre, 2006), no. 1.4) [10]

It behoveth the loved ones of God to occupy themselves under all circumstances with that which is conducive to the edification of human souls, the advancement of the world of being, and the exaltation of the Word of God, the realization of which dependeth upon the deliberations of the trustees of the House of Justice. Well is it with them that strive to render service to the world of humanity. The influence of these souls will lead the world from hardship to comfort, from poverty to wealth, and from abasement to glory.

(Bahá'u'lláh, from a Tablet—translated from the Persian) [11]

3

Once in session, it behoveth them to converse, on behalf of God's servants, upon the affairs and interests of all. . . . In like manner, they should consider such matters as the refinement of manners, the preservation of human dignity, the development of cities, and the polity which God hath made a bulwark for His lands and a fortress for His people.

(Bahá'u'lláh, from a Tablet—translated from the Persian) [12]

God has given us eyes, that we may look about us at the world, and lay hold of whatsoever will further civilization and the arts of living. He has given us ears, that we may hear and profit by the wisdom of scholars and philosophers and arise to promote and practice it. Senses and faculties have been bestowed upon us, to be devoted to the service of the general good; so that we, distinguished above all other forms of life for perceptiveness and reason, should labor at all times and along all lines, whether the occasion be great or small, ordinary or extraordinary, until all mankind are safely gathered into the impregnable stronghold of knowledge. We should continually be establishing new bases for human happiness and creating and promoting new instrumentalities toward this end. How excellent, how honorable is man if he arises to fulfill his responsibilities; how wretched and contemptible, if he shuts his eyes to the welfare of society and wastes his precious life in pursuing his own selfish interests and personal advantages. Supreme happiness is man's, and he beholds the signs of God in the world and in the human soul, if he urges on the steed of high endeavor in the arena of civilization and justice.

('Abdu'l-Bahá, *The Secret of Divine Civilization* (Wilmette: Bahá'í Publishing, 2007), ¶6) [13]

Exert every effort in the fields of development and of civilization, in the acquisition of knowledge, the increase of trade, the improvement of agriculture and the promotion of modern discoveries.

('Abdu'l-Bahá, from a Tablet—translated from the Persian) [14]

Guide and counsel at all times the friends of God, one and all, to be occupied day and night with that which is conducive to Iran's abiding glory, and to exert the utmost effort and the greatest endeavour in order to refine character and manners, labour assiduously, aim for lofty goals, promote love and affection, and foster the progress and development of industry, agriculture and trade.

('Abdu'l-Bahá, from a Tablet—translated from the Persian) [15]

The friends must engage in the work of developing Persia, that is, they must exert great efforts in the promotion of agriculture, industry, trade, education, arts, and sciences.

('Abdu'l-Bahá, from a Tablet—translated from the Persian) [16]

And now, in gratitude for the assistance, confirmation, protection, and loving-kindness vouchsafed by the All-Glorious Lord, the beloved of God must with great wisdom strive to strengthen the pillars of the Cause of God, to establish and promote the religion of God, to diffuse the fragrances of God, and to exalt the Word of God. They must exert every effort for the advancement of the souls in all stages of existence. They must educate the children and teach them useful arts, reach ever higher degrees of civilization, multiply national crafts and industry, promote trade, improve agriculture, provide learning for all, educate women and honour them, and show consideration for the handmaidens of God. They must strive with heart and soul to create love and unity among the friends, to serve the government, and to be true to the royal throne, the well-wishers of everyone, and obedient to the valiant sovereign.

('Abdu'l-Bahá, from a Tablet—translated from the Persian) [17]

The matter of Teaching, its direction, its ways and means, its extension, its consolidation, essential as they are to the interests of the Cause, constitute by no means the only issue which should receive the full attention of these Assemblies. A careful study of Bahá'u'lláh's and 'Abdu'l-Bahá's Tablets will reveal that other duties, no less vital to the interests of the Cause, devolve upon the elected representatives of the friends in every locality. . . .

They must do their utmost to extend at all times the helping hand to the poor, the sick, the disabled, the orphan, the widow, irrespective of color, caste and creed.

They must promote by every means in their power the material as well as the spiritual enlightenment of youth, the means for the education of children, institute, whenever possible, Bahá'í educational institutions, organize and supervise their work and provide the best means for their progress and development. . . .

They must undertake the arrangement of the regular meetings of the friends, the feasts and the anniversaries, as well as the special gatherings designed to serve and promote the social, intellectual and spiritual interests of their fellow-men.

(Shoghi Effendi, from a letter dated 12 March 1923, in *Bahá'í Administration: Selected Messages, 1922–1932* (Wilmette: Bahá'í Publishing Trust, 1974), pp. 37–38) [18]

From the beginning of His stupendous mission, Bahá'u'lláh urged upon the attention of nations the necessity of ordering human affairs in such a way as to bring into being a world unified in all the essential aspects of its life. In unnumbered verses and tablets He repeatedly and variously declared the "progress of the world" and the "development of nations" as being among the ordinances of God for this day. The oneness of mankind, which is at once the operating principle and ultimate goal of His Revelation, implies the achievement of a dynamic coherence between the spiritual and practical requirements of life on earth. The indispensability of this coherence is unmistakably illustrated in His ordination of the Mashriqu'l-Adhkár, the spiritual centre of every Bahá'í community round which must flourish dependencies dedicated to the social, humanitarian, educational and scientific advancement of mankind. Thus, we can readily appreciate that although it has hitherto been impracticable for Bahá'í institutions generally to emphasize development activities, the concept of social and economic development is enshrined in the sacred Teachings of our Faith. The beloved Master, through His illuminating words and deeds, set the example for the application of this concept to the reconstruction of society. Witness, for instance, what social and economic progress the Iranian believers attained under His loving guidance and, subsequently, with the unfailing encouragement of the Guardian of the Cause.

(The Universal House of Justice, from a message dated 20 October 1983 to the Bahá'ís of the World) [19]

'Abdu'l-Bahá has extolled "two calls" to "success and prosperity" that can be heard from the "heights of the happiness of mankind." One is the call of "civilization," of "progress of the material world." It comprises the "laws," "regulations," "arts and sciences" through which humanity develops. The other is the "soul-stirring call of God," on which depends the eternal happiness of humanity. "This second call," the Master has explained, "is founded upon the instructions and exhortations of the Lord and the admonitions and altruistic emotions belonging to the realm of morality which, like unto a brilliant light, brighten and illumine the lamp of the realities of mankind. Its penetrative power is the Word of God." As you continue to labour in your clusters, you will be drawn further and further into the life of the society around you and will be challenged to extend the process of systematic learning in which you are engaged to encompass a growing range of human endeavours. In the approaches you take, the methods you adopt, and the instruments you employ, you will need to achieve the same degree of coherence that characterizes the pattern of growth presently under way.

(The Universal House of Justice, Riḍván 2008 message to the Bahá'ís of the World) [20]

The term "politics" can have a broad meaning, and therefore it is important to distinguish between partisan political activity and the discourse and action intended to bring about constructive social change. While the former is proscribed, the latter is enjoined; indeed, a central purpose of the Bahá'í community is social transformation. 'Abdu'l-Bahá's treatise *The Secret of Divine Civilization* amply demonstrates the Faith's commitment to promoting social change without entering into the arena of partisan politics. So too, innumerable passages in the Bahá'í Writings encourage the believers to contribute to the betterment of the world. "Be anxiously concerned with the needs of the age ye live in," Bahá'u'lláh states, "and center your deliberations on its exigencies and requirements." 'Abdu'l-Bahá urges the friends to "become distinguished in all the virtues of the human world—for faithfulness and sincerity, for justice and fidelity, for firmness and steadfastness, for philanthropic deeds and service to the human world, for love toward every human being, for unity and accord with all people, for removing prejudices and promoting international peace." Further, in a letter written on his behalf, Shoghi Effendi explains that "much as the friends must guard against in any way seeming to identify themselves or the Cause with any political party, they must also guard against the other extreme of never taking part, with other progressive groups, in conferences or committees designed to promote some activity in entire accord with our teachings." In another letter written on his behalf in 1948, when racial inequality was enshrined in the laws of many states in the United States, he indicates that there is "no objection at all to the students taking part in something so obviously akin to the spirit of our teachings as a campus demonstration against race prejudice." Bahá'ís must, therefore, be tireless in addressing, through word and deed, a range of social issues.

(From a letter dated 23 December 2008 written on behalf of the Universal House of Justice to an individual believer)   [21]

Collective Maturity and an Ever-Advancing Civilization

All men have been created to carry forward an ever-advancing civilization.

(Bahá'u'lláh, *Gleanings from the Writings of Bahá'u'lláh* (Wilmette: Bahá'í Publishing Trust, 1983), no. 109.2)   [22]

All men have been called into being for the betterment of the world. It behoveth every soul to arise and serve his brethren for the sake of God.

(Bahá'u'lláh, *The Tabernacle of Unity*, no. 2.42)   [23]

And the honor and distinction of the individual consist in this, that he among all the world's multitudes should become a source of social good. Is any larger bounty conceivable than this, that an individual, looking within himself, should find that by the confirming grace of God he has become the cause of peace and well-being, of happiness

9

and advantage to his fellow men? No, by the one true God, there is no greater bliss, no more complete delight.

('Abdu'l-Bahá, *The Secret of Divine Civilization*, ¶5)   [24]

O namesake of the Chaste One![1] The sea of bounty hath surged so high as to flood the shores of existence with the waters of infinite grace. The world of being hath therefore been set in wondrous motion and hath been revived and blessed. Minds have soared to new heights, understanding hath increased, movement hath become rapid, and progress hath become powerfully evident in all aspects of life. Thus, great discoveries have been made, mighty enterprises have been established, wonderful inventions have appeared, and the mysteries of the universe have stepped forth from the invisible plane into the realm of the visible. Wherefore must the friends, one and all, exhibit a signal effort to create a new invention, discover a new science, engage in a great enterprise, or manifest a power or a bestowal in the human world. I beseech God that thou mayest be assisted and confirmed under all conditions. The Glory of Glories rest upon thee.

('Abdu'l-Bahá, from a Tablet—translated from the Persian) [25]

All created things have their degree, or stage, of maturity. The period of maturity in the life of a tree is the time of its fruit bearing. The maturity of a plant is the time of its blossoming and flower. The animal attains a stage of full growth and completeness, and in the human kingdom man reaches his maturity when the lights of intelligence have their greatest power and development. . . .

---

1. i.e., Yaḥyá, the Arabic name of John the Baptist, who was titled "the Chaste." See Qur'án 3:39.

10

Similarly, there are periods and stages in the life of the aggregate world of humanity, which at one time was passing through its degree of childhood, at another its time of youth but now has entered its long presaged period of maturity, the evidences of which are everywhere visible and apparent. Therefore, the requirements and conditions of former periods have changed and merged into exigencies which distinctly characterize the present age of the world of mankind. That which was applicable to human needs during the early history of the race could neither meet nor satisfy the demands of this day and period of newness and consummation. Humanity has emerged from its former degrees of limitation and preliminary training. Man must now become imbued with new virtues and powers, new moralities, new capacities. New bounties, bestowals and perfections are awaiting and already descending upon him. The gifts and graces of the period of youth, although timely and sufficient during the adolescence of the world of mankind, are now incapable of meeting the requirements of its maturity.

('Abdu'l-Bahá, *The Promulgation of Universal Peace: Talks Delivered by 'Abdu'l-Bahá during His Visit to the United States and Canada in 1912* (Wilmette: Bahá'í Publishing, 2012), pp. 617–18) [26]

"The heights," Bahá'u'lláh Himself testifies, "which, through the most gracious favor of God, mortal man can attain in this Day are as yet unrevealed to his sight. The world of being hath never had, nor doth it yet possess, the capacity for such a revelation. The day, however, is approaching when the potentialities of so great a favor will, by virtue of His behest, be manifested unto men."

For the revelation of so great a favor a period of intense turmoil and wide-spread suffering would seem to be indispensable. Resplendent as has been the Age that has witnessed the inception of the Mission with which Bahá'u'lláh has been entrusted, the interval which must elapse ere that Age yields its choicest fruit must, it is becoming increasingly apparent, be overshadowed by such moral and social gloom as can alone prepare an unrepentant humanity for the prize she is destined to inherit.

Into such a period we are now steadily and irresistibly moving. Amidst the shadows which are increasingly gathering about us we can faintly discern the glimmerings of Bahá'u'lláh's unearthly sovereignty appearing fitfully on the horizon of history. To us, the "generation of the half-light," living at a time which may be designated as the period of the incubation of the World Commonwealth envisaged by Bahá'u'lláh, has been assigned a task whose high privilege we can never sufficiently appreciate, and the arduousness of which we can as yet but dimly recognize. We may well believe, we who are called upon to experience the operation of the dark forces destined to unloose a flood of agonizing afflictions, that the darkest hour that must precede the dawn of the Golden Age of our Faith has not yet struck. Deep as is the gloom that already encircles the world, the afflictive ordeals which that world is to suffer are still in preparation, nor can their blackness be as yet imagined. We stand on the threshold of an age whose convulsions proclaim alike the death-pangs of the old order and the birth-pangs of the new. Through the generating influence of the Faith announced by Bahá'u'lláh this New World Order may be said to have been conceived. We can, at the present moment, experience its stirrings in the womb of a travailing age—an age waiting for the appointed hour at which it can cast its burden and yield its fairest fruit.

(Shoghi Effendi, from a letter dated 11 March 1936, in *The World Order of Bahá'u'lláh: Selected Letters* (Wilmette: Bahá'í Publishing Trust, 1991), pp. 168–69) [27]

As we view the world around us, we are compelled to observe the manifold evidences of that universal fermentation which, in every continent of the globe and in every department of human life, be it religious, social, economic or political, is purging and reshaping humanity in anticipation of the Day when the wholeness of the human race will have been recognized and its unity established. A twofold process, however, can be distinguished, each tending, in its own way and with an accelerated momentum, to bring to a climax the forces that are transforming the face of our planet. The first is essentially an integrating process, while the second is fundamentally disruptive. The former, as it steadily evolves, unfolds a System which may well serve as a pattern for that world polity towards which a strangely-disordered world is continually advancing; while the latter, as its disintegrating influence deepens, tends to tear down, with increasing violence, the antiquated barriers that seek to block humanity's progress towards its destined goal. The constructive process stands associated with the nascent Faith of Bahá'u'lláh, and is the harbinger of the New World Order that Faith must erelong establish. The destructive forces that characterize the other should be identified with a civilization that has refused to answer to the expectation of a new age, and is consequently falling into chaos and decline.

(Shoghi Effendi, from a letter dated 11 March 1936, in *The World Order of Bahá'u'lláh*, p. 170) [28]

The long ages of infancy and childhood, through which the human race had to pass, have receded into the background. Humanity is now experiencing the commotions invariably associated with the most turbulent stage of its evolution, the stage of adolescence, when the impetuosity of youth and its vehemence reach their climax, and must gradually be superseded by the calmness, the wisdom, and the maturity that characterize the stage of manhood. Then will the human race reach that stature of ripeness which will enable it to acquire all the powers and capacities upon which its ultimate development must depend.

(Shoghi Effendi, from a letter dated 11 March 1936, in *The World Order of Bahá'u'lláh*, p. 202)   [29]

Of the principles enshrined in these Tablets the most vital of them all is the principle of the oneness and wholeness of the human race, which may well be regarded as the hall-mark of Bahá'u'lláh's Revelation and the pivot of His teachings. . . . "We, verily," He declares, "have come to unite and weld together all that dwell on earth." "So potent is the light of unity," He further states, "that it can illuminate the whole earth." . . . Unity, He states, is the goal that "excelleth every goal" and an aspiration which is "the monarch of all aspirations." "The world," He proclaims, "is but one country, and mankind its citizens." He further affirms that the unification of mankind, the last stage in the evolution of humanity towards maturity is inevitable, that "soon will the present day order be rolled up, and a new one spread out in its stead," that "the whole earth is now in a state of pregnancy," that "the day is approaching when it will have yielded its noblest fruits, when from it will have sprung forth the loftiest trees, the most enchanting blossoms, the most heavenly blessings." He deplores the defectiveness of the prevailing order, exposes the inadequacy of patriotism as a directing and controlling force in human society, and regards the "love of mankind" and service to its interests as the worthiest and most laudable objects of human endeavor.

(Shoghi Effendi, *God Passes By* (Wilmette: Bahá'í Publishing Trust, 1974, 2019 printing), pp. 343–44)   [30]

Inseparable from the Bahá'í perspective on politics is a particular conception of history, its course and direction. Humanity, it is the firm conviction of every follower of Bahá'u'lláh, is approaching today the crowning stage in a millennia-long process which has brought it from its collective infancy to the threshold of maturity—a stage that will witness the unification of the human race. Not unlike the individual who passes through the unsettled yet promising period of adolescence, during which latent powers and capacities come to light, humankind as a whole is in the midst of an unprecedented transition. Behind so much of the turbulence and commotion of contemporary life are the fits and starts of a humanity struggling to come of age. Widely accepted practices and conventions, cherished attitudes and habits, are one by one being rendered obsolete, as the imperatives of maturity begin to assert themselves.

Bahá'ís are encouraged to see in the revolutionary changes taking place in every sphere of life the interaction of two fundamental processes. One is destructive in nature, while the other is integrative; both serve to carry humanity, each in its own way, along the path leading towards its full maturity. The operation of the former is everywhere apparent—in the vicissitudes that have afflicted time-honoured institutions, in the impotence of leaders at all levels to mend the fractures appearing in the structure of society, in the dismantling of social norms that have long held in check unseemly passions, and in the despondency and indifference exhibited not only by individuals but also by entire societies that have lost any vital sense of purpose. Though devastating in their effects, the forces of disintegration tend to sweep away barriers that block humanity's progress, opening space for the process of integration to draw diverse groups together and disclosing new opportunities for cooperation and collaboration. Bahá'ís, of course, strive to align themselves, individually and collectively, with forces associated with the process of integration, which, they are confident, will continue to gain in strength, no matter how bleak the immediate horizons. Human affairs will be utterly reorganized, and an era of universal peace inaugurated. . . .

. . . Animating the Bahá'í effort to discover the nature of a new set of relationships among these three protagonists [the individual, the institutions, and the community] is a vision of a future society that derives inspiration from the analogy drawn by Bahá'u'lláh, in a Tablet penned nearly a century and a half ago, which compares the world to the human body. Cooperation is the principle that governs the functioning of that system. Just as the appearance of the rational soul in this realm of existence is made possible through the complex association of countless cells, whose organization in tissues and organs allows for the realization of distinctive capacities, so can civilization be seen as the outcome of a set of interactions among closely integrated, diverse components which have transcended the narrow purpose of tending to their own existence. And just as the viability of every cell and every organ is contingent upon the health of the body as a whole, so should the prosperity of every individual, every family, every people be sought in the well-being of the entire human race.

(The Universal House of Justice, from a message dated 2 March 2013 to the Bahá'ís of Iran)   [31]

Oneness and Justice

. . . The light of men is Justice. Quench it not with the contrary winds of oppression and tyranny. The purpose of justice is the appearance of unity among men. . . .

. . . Shut your eyes to estrangement, then fix your gaze upon unity. Cleave tenaciously unto that which will lead to the well-being and tranquility of all mankind. This span of earth is but one homeland and one habitation. It behooveth you to abandon vainglory which causeth alienation and to set your hearts on whatever will ensure harmony.

(Bahá'u'lláh, *Tablets of Bahá'u'lláh Revealed after the Kitáb-i-Aqdas*, pp. 66–68)   [32]

The Great Being saith: O well-beloved ones! The tabernacle of unity hath been raised; regard ye not one another as strangers. Ye are the fruits of one tree, and the leaves of one branch. We cherish the hope that the light of justice may shine upon the world and sanctify it from tyranny. If the rulers and kings of the earth, the symbols of the power of God, exalted be His glory, arise and resolve to dedicate themselves to whatever will promote the highest interests of the whole of humanity, the reign of justice will assuredly be established amongst the children of men, and the effulgence of its light will envelop the whole earth. . . .

. . . There is no force on earth that can equal in its conquering power the force of justice and wisdom. I, verily, affirm that there is not, and hath never been, a host more mighty than that of justice and wisdom. . . . There can be no doubt whatever that if the daystar of justice, which the clouds of tyranny have obscured, were to shed its light upon men, the face of the earth would be completely transformed.

(Bahá'u'lláh, *Tablets of Bahá'u'lláh Revealed after the Kitáb-i-Aqdas*, pp. 164–65)   [33]

We entreat God to deliver the light of equity and the sun of justice from the thick clouds of waywardness, and cause them to shine forth upon men. No light can compare with the light of justice. The establishment of order in the world and the tranquility of the nations depend upon it.

(Bahá'u'lláh, *Epistle to the Son of the Wolf* (Wilmette: Bahá'í Publishing Trust, 1988), pp. 28–29)   [34]

The second attribute of perfection is justice and impartiality. This means to have no regard for one's own personal benefits and selfish advantages, and to carry out the laws of God without the slightest concern for anything else. It means to see one's self as only one of the servants of God, the All-Possessing, and except for aspiring to spiritual distinction, never attempting to be singled out from the others. It means to consider the welfare of the community as one's own. It means, in brief, to regard humanity as a single individual, and one's own self as a member of that corporeal form, and to know of a certainty that if pain or injury afflicts any member of that body, it must inevitably result in suffering for all the rest.

('Abdu'l-Bahá, *The Secret of Divine Civilization*, ¶71)   [35]

O ye beloved of God! Know ye, verily, that the happiness of mankind lieth in the unity and the harmony of the human race, and that spiritual and material developments are conditioned upon love and amity among all men.

('Abdu'l-Bahá, *Selections from the Writings of 'Abdu'l-Bahá* (Wilmette: Bahá'í Publishing Trust, 1997, 2009 printing), no. 225.10)   [36]

O well-wisher of the world of humanity! Praised be God that thine intention was good, that thou didst acquire knowledge and learning, and that thy wish is to engage in service to the peoples of the world. I beseech God that thou mayest succeed in this purpose and mayest manifest that which lieth concealed within thy heart. In the world of creation, good intentions are of two kinds. One kind is particular and aimed at specific people; this is limited and its scope is extremely narrow. The other kind is directed towards all created things; it is all-pervading and extensive in range. Whatsoever is undertaken for the sake of the universal good is of God. Therefore, undertakings that relate somewhat to the general good may be accomplished among civilized nations, but the only thing that is directed wholly towards the general good is the Word of God and Divine wisdom. This is the power which can effect a fundamental change and transformation in the world of being. This force is creative; it is generative and revitalizing and bringeth forth a new creation. Exert thine utmost endeavour, therefore, in pursuing that which will be the cause of progress of the world of humanity and will lead to perpetual exaltation and eternal life. Upon thee be greetings and praise.

('Abdu'l-Bahá, from a Tablet—translated from the Persian) [37]

Let there be no mistake. The principle of the Oneness of Mankind—the pivot round which all the teachings of Bahá'u'lláh revolve—is no mere outburst of ignorant emotionalism or an expression of vague and pious hope. . . . Its message is applicable not only to the individual, but concerns itself primarily with the nature of those essential relationships that must bind all the states and nations as members of one human family. It does not constitute merely the enunciation of an ideal, but stands inseparably associated with an institution adequate to embody its truth, demonstrate its validity, and perpetuate its influence. It implies an organic change in the structure of present-day society, a change such as the world has not yet experienced. It constitutes a challenge, at once bold and universal, to outworn shibboleths of national creeds—creeds that have had their day and which must, in the ordinary course of events as shaped and controlled by Providence, give way to a new gospel, fundamentally different from, and infinitely superior to, what the world has already conceived. It calls for no less than the reconstruction and the demilitarization of the whole civilized world—a world organically unified in all the essential aspects of its life, its political machinery, its spiritual aspiration, its trade and finance, its script and language, and yet infinite in the diversity of the national characteristics of its federated units.

(Shoghi Effendi, from a letter dated 28 November 1931, in *The World Order of Bahá'u'lláh*, pp. 42–43)   [38]

Their Faith they conceive to be essentially non-political, supra-national in character, rigidly non-partisan, and entirely dissociated from nationalistic ambitions, pursuits, and purposes. Such a Faith knows no division of class or of party. It subordinates, without hesitation or equivo-cation, every particularistic interest, be it personal, regional, or national, to the paramount interests of humanity, firmly convinced that in a world of inter-dependent peoples and nations the advantage of the part is best to be reached by the advantage of the whole, and that no abiding benefit can be conferred upon the component parts if the general interests of the entity itself are ignored or neglected.

(Shoghi Effendi, from a letter dated 11 March 1936, in *The World Order of Bahá'u'lláh*, p. 198)   [39]

Unification of the whole of mankind is the hall-mark of the stage which human society is now approaching. Unity of family, of tribe, of city-state, and nation have been successively attempted and fully estab-lished. World unity is the goal towards which a harassed humanity is striving. Nation-building has come to an end. The anarchy inherent in state sovereignty is moving towards a climax. A world, growing to maturity, must abandon this fetish, recognize the oneness and whole-ness of human relationships, and establish once for all the machinery that can best incarnate this fundamental principle of its life.

(Shoghi Effendi, from a letter dated 11 March 1936, in *The World Order of Bahá'u'lláh*, p. 202)   [40]

Unbridled nationalism, as distinguished from a sane and legitimate patriotism, must give way to a wider loyalty, to the love of humanity as a whole. Bahá'u'lláh's statement is: "The earth is but one country, and mankind its citizens." The concept of world citizenship is a direct result of the contraction of the world into a single neighbourhood through scientific advances and of the indisputable interdependence of nations. Love of all the world's peoples does not exclude love of one's country. The advantage of the part in a world society is best served by promoting the advantage of the whole.

(The Universal House of Justice, from a message dated October 1985 to the Peoples of the World) [41]

... not only are humanity's talents and capacities shared by all its members, but its problems and afflictions likewise ultimately affect all. Whether in sickness or health, the human family constitutes a single species, and the condition of any part of it cannot be intelligently considered in isolation from this systemic oneness. As the present state of the world illustrates all too clearly, attempts by the leadership of society to proceed otherwise is merely to exacerbate the problems.

(From a letter dated 27 November 2001 written on behalf of the Universal House of Justice to an individual believer) [42]

Penetrating, indeed, is Shoghi Effendi's depiction of the process of disintegration accelerating in the world. Equally striking is the accuracy with which he analysed the forces associated with the process of integration. He spoke of a "gradual diffusion of the spirit of world solidarity which is spontaneously arising out of the welter of a disorganized society" as an indirect manifestation of Bahá'u'lláh's conception of the principle of the oneness of humankind. This spirit of solidarity has continued to spread over the decades, and today its effect is apparent in a range of developments, from the rejection of deeply ingrained racial prejudices to the dawning consciousness of world citizenship, from heightened environmental awareness to collaborative efforts in the promotion of public health, from the concern for human rights to the systematic pursuit of universal education, from the establishment of interfaith activities to the efflorescence of hundreds of thousands of local, national and international organizations engaged in some form of social action.

(The Universal House of Justice, Riḍván 2006 message to the Bahá'ís of the World)   [43]

The organized endeavors of the Bahá'í community in these areas are reinforced by the diverse initiatives of individual believers working in various fields—as volunteers, professionals, and experts—to contribute to social change. The distinctive nature of their approach is to avoid conflict and the contest for power while striving to unite people in the search for underlying moral and spiritual principles and for practical measures that can lead to the just resolution of the problems afflicting society. Bahá'ís perceive humanity as a single body. All are inseparably bound to one another. A social order structured to meet the needs of one group at the expense of another results in injustice and oppression. Instead, the best interest of each component part is achieved by considering its needs in the context of the well-being of the whole.

(From a letter dated 23 December 2008 written on behalf of the Universal House of Justice to an individual believer)   [44]

As you know from your study of the Bahá'í writings, the principle that is to infuse all facets of organized life on the planet is the oneness of humankind, the hallmark of the age of maturity. That humanity constitutes a single people is a truth that, once viewed with skepticism, claims widespread acceptance today. The rejection of deeply ingrained prejudices and a growing sense of world citizenship are among the signs of this heightened awareness. Yet, however promising the rise in collective consciousness may be, it should be seen as only the first step of a process that will take decades—nay, centuries—to unfold. For the principle of the oneness of humankind, as proclaimed by Bahá'u'lláh, asks not merely for cooperation among people and nations. It calls for a complete reconceptualization of the relationships that sustain society. The deepening environmental crisis, driven by a system that condones the pillage of natural resources to satisfy an insatiable thirst for more, suggests how entirely inadequate is the present conception of humanity's relationship with nature; the deterioration of the home environment, with the accompanying rise in the systematic exploitation of women and children worldwide, makes clear how pervasive are the misbegotten notions that define relations within the family unit; the persistence of despotism, on the one hand, and the increasing disregard for authority, on the other, reveal how unsatisfactory to a maturing humanity is the current relationship between the individual and the institutions of society; the concentration of material wealth in the hands of a minority of the world's population gives an indication of how fundamentally ill-conceived are relationships among the many sectors of what is now an emerging global community. The principle of the oneness of humankind implies, then, an organic change in the very structure of society.

(The Universal House of Justice, from a message dated 2 March 2013 to the Bahá'ís of Iran) [45]

. . . though world unity is possible—nay, inevitable—it ultimately cannot be achieved without unreserved acceptance of the oneness of humankind, described by the Guardian as "the pivot round which all the teachings of Bahá'u'lláh revolve." With what insight and eloquence did he expound upon the far-reaching implications of this cardinal principle! Plainly he saw, amidst the turbulence of world affairs, how the reality that humanity is one people must be the starting point for a new order. The vast array of relations among nations—and within them—all need to be re-envisaged in this light.

The realization of such a vision will require, sooner or later, an historic feat of statesmanship from the leaders of the world. Alas, the will to attempt this feat is still wanting. Humanity is gripped by a crisis of identity, as various peoples and groups struggle to define themselves, their place in the world, and how they should act. Without a vision of shared identity and common purpose, they fall into competing ideologies and power struggles. Seemingly countless permutations of "us" and "them" define group identities ever more narrowly and in contrast to one another. Over time, this splintering into divergent interest groups has weakened the cohesion of society itself. Rival conceptions about the primacy of a particular people are peddled to the exclusion of the truth that humanity is on a common journey in which all are protagonists. Consider how radically different such a fragmented conception of human identity is from the one that follows from a recognition of the oneness of humanity. In this perspective, the diversity that characterizes the human family, far from contradicting its oneness, endows it with richness. Unity, in its Bahá'í expression, contains the essential concept of diversity, distinguishing it from uniformity. It is through love for all people, and by subordinating lesser loyalties to the best interests of humankind, that the unity of the world can be realized and the infinite expressions of human diversity find their highest fulfilment.

(The Universal House of Justice, from a message dated 18 January 2019 to the Bahá'ís of the World)   [46]

The Role of Knowledge

Knowledge is one of the wondrous gifts of God. It is incumbent upon everyone to acquire it. Such arts and material means as are now manifest have been achieved by virtue of His knowledge and wisdom which have been revealed in Epistles and Tablets through His Most Exalted Pen—a Pen out of whose treasury pearls of wisdom and utterance and the arts and crafts of the world are brought to light.

(Bahá'u'lláh, *Tablets of Bahá'u'lláh Revealed after the Kitáb-i-Aqdas*, p. 39)   [47]

Knowledge is as wings to man's life, and a ladder for his ascent. Its acquisition is incumbent upon everyone. The knowledge of such sciences, however, should be acquired as can profit the peoples of the earth, and not those which begin with words and end with words. . . . In truth, knowledge is a veritable treasure for man, and a source of glory, of bounty, of joy, of exaltation, of cheer and gladness unto him.

(Bahá'u'lláh, *Tablets of Bahá'u'lláh Revealed after the Kitáb-i-Aqdas*, pp. 51–52)   [48]

The Great Being saith: The learned of the day must direct the people to acquire those branches of knowledge which are of use, that both the learned themselves and the generality of mankind may derive benefits therefrom. Such academic pursuits as begin and end in words alone have never been and will never be of any worth.

(Bahá'u'lláh, *Tablets of Bahá'u'lláh Revealed after the Kitáb-i-Aqdas*, p. 169)   [49]

In this day the choicest fruit of the tree of knowledge is that which serveth the welfare of humanity and safeguardeth its interests.

(Bahá'u'lláh, *The Tabernacle of Unity*, no. 1.16)   [50]

Strain every nerve to acquire both inner and outer perfections, for the fruit of the human tree hath ever been and will ever be perfections both within and without. It is not desirable that a man be left without knowledge or skills, for he is then but a barren tree. Then, so much as capacity and capability allow, ye needs must deck the tree of being with fruits such as knowledge, wisdom, spiritual perception and eloquent speech.

(Bahá'u'lláh, from a Tablet—translated from the Persian) [51]

. . . every branch of learning, conjoined with the love of God, is approved and worthy of praise; but bereft of His love, learning is barren—indeed, it bringeth on madness. Every kind of knowledge, every science, is as a tree: if the fruit of it be the love of God, then is it a blessed tree, but if not, that tree is but dried-up wood, and shall only feed the fire.

('Abdu'l-Bahá, *Selections from the Writings of 'Abdu'l-Bahá*, no. 154.3) [52]

Make every effort to acquire the advanced knowledge of the day, and strain every nerve to carry forward the divine civilization.

('Abdu'l-Bahá, from a Tablet—translated from the Persian) [53]

Good behaviour and high moral character must come first, for unless the character be trained, acquiring knowledge will only prove injurious. Knowledge is praiseworthy when it is coupled with ethical conduct and virtuous character; otherwise it is a deadly poison, a frightful danger. A physician of evil character, and who betrayeth his trust, can bring on death, and become the source of numerous infirmities and diseases.

('Abdu'l-Bahá, from a Tablet—translated from the Persian) [54]

The harder they strive to widen the scope of their knowledge, the better and more gratifying will be the result. Let the loved ones of God, whether young or old, whether male or female, each according to his capabilities, bestir themselves and spare no efforts to acquire the various current branches of knowledge, both spiritual and secular, and of the arts. Whensoever they gather in their meetings let their conversation be confined to learned subjects and to information on the knowledge of the day.

('Abdu'l-Bahá, from a Tablet—translated from the Arabic) [55]

It is clear that learning is the greatest bestowal of God; that knowledge and the acquirement thereof is a blessing from Heaven. Thus is it incumbent upon the friends of God to exert such an effort and strive with such eagerness to promote divine knowledge, culture and the sciences, that erelong those who are schoolchildren today will become the most erudite of all the fraternity of the wise. This is a service rendered unto God Himself, and it is one of His inescapable commandments.

('Abdu'l-Bahá, from a Tablet—translated from the Persian) [56]

. . . the religion of God is the promoter of truth, the establisher of science and learning, the supporter of knowledge, the civilizer of the human race, the discoverer of the secrets of existence, and the enlightener of the horizons of the world. How then could it oppose knowledge? God forbid! On the contrary, in the sight of God knowledge is the greatest human virtue and the noblest human perfection. To oppose knowledge is pure ignorance, and he who abhors knowledge and learning is not a human being but a mindless animal. For knowledge is light, life, felicity, perfection, and beauty, and causes the soul to draw nigh to the divine threshold. It is the honour and glory of the human realm and the greatest of God's bounties. Knowledge is identical to guidance, and ignorance is the essence of error.

Happy are those who spend their days in the pursuit of knowledge, in the discovery of the secrets of the universe, and in the meticulous investigation of truth!

('Abdu'l-Bahá, *Some Answered Questions* (Haifa: Bahá'í World Centre, 2014), no. 34.9–10) [57]

All the sciences, branches of learning, arts, inventions, institutions, undertakings, and discoveries have resulted from the comprehension of the rational soul. These were once impenetrable secrets, hidden mysteries, and unknown realities, and the rational soul gradually discovered them and brought them out of the invisible plane into the realm of the visible. This is the greatest power of comprehension in the world of nature, and the uttermost limit of its flight is to comprehend the realities, signs, and properties of contingent things.

('Abdu'l-Bahá, *Some Answered Questions*, no. 58.3) [58]

Science is the first emanation from God toward man. All created beings embody the potentiality of material perfection, but the power of intellectual investigation and scientific acquisition is a higher virtue specialized to man alone. Other beings and organisms are deprived of this potentiality and attainment. God has created or deposited this love of reality in man. The development and progress of a nation is according to the measure and degree of that nation's scientific attainments. Through this means its greatness is continually increased, and day by day the welfare and prosperity of its people are assured.

('Abdu'l-Bahá, *The Promulgation of Universal Peace*, p. 67) [59]

All the heavenly Books, divine Prophets, sages and philosophers agree that warfare is destructive to human development, and peace constructive. They agree that war and strife strike at the foundations of humanity. Therefore, a power is needed to prevent war and to proclaim and establish the oneness of humanity.

But knowledge of the need of this power is not sufficient. Realizing that wealth is desirable is not becoming wealthy. The admission that scientific attainment is praiseworthy does not confer scientific knowledge. Acknowledgment of the excellence of honor does not make a man honorable. Knowledge of human conditions and the needed remedy for them is not the cause of their betterment. To admit that health is good does not constitute health. A skilled physician is needed to remedy existing human conditions. As a physician is required to have complete knowledge of pathology, diagnosis, therapeutics and treatment, so this World Physician must be wise, skillful and capable before health will result. His mere knowledge is not health; it must be applied and the remedy carried out.

The attainment of any object is conditioned upon knowledge, volition and action. Unless these three conditions are forthcoming, there is no execution or accomplishment.

('Abdu'l-Bahá, *The Promulgation of Universal Peace*, pp. 217–18)
[60]

Acceptance of the teachings of Bahá'u'lláh carries with it the commitment to strive for individual spiritual maturity and to participate in collective efforts to build a thriving society and contribute to the common weal. Science and religion are the two inseparable, reciprocal systems of knowledge impelling the advancement of civilization. In the words of 'Abdu'l-Bahá, "The progress of the world of humanity dependeth upon knowledge, and its decline is due to ignorance. When the human race gaineth in knowledge it becometh heavenly, and when it acquireth learning it taketh on lordly attributes." To seek to acquire knowledge and learning and to study useful sciences and crafts are among the fundamental beliefs of the followers of Bahá'u'lláh. There-fore, the long-term solution you have chosen as a means of counteract-ing the difficulties imposed upon you in the path of higher education is to engage in constructive collaboration with other proponents of peace and reconciliation to build a progressive and orderly society committed to the promotion of knowledge and social justice.

(The Universal House of Justice, from a message dated 17 June 2011 to the Believers in the Cradle of the Faith) [61]

One of the critical aspects of a conceptual framework that will require careful attention in the years ahead is the generation and application of knowledge. . . . At the heart of most disciplines of human knowledge is a degree of consensus about methodology—an understanding of methods and how to use them appropriately to systematically investi-gate reality to achieve reliable results and sound conclusions. Bahá'ís who are involved in various disciplines—economics, education, his-tory, social science, philosophy, and many others—are obviously con-versant and fully engaged with the methods employed in their fields. It is they who have the responsibility to earnestly strive to reflect on the implications that the truths found in the Revelation may hold for their work. The principle of the harmony of science and religion, faithfully upheld, will ensure that religious belief does not succumb to supersti-tion and that scientific findings are not appropriated by materialism.

(From a letter dated 24 July 2013 written on behalf of the Uni-versal House of Justice to a National Spiritual Assembly) [62]

Fundamentally, a great share of the Bahá'í community's efforts has been directed at addressing the root cause of religious prejudice—ignorance. "The perpetuation of ignorance," the House of Justice has stated, "is a most grievous form of oppression; it reinforces the many walls of prejudice that stand as barriers to the realization of the oneness of humankind. . . . Access to knowledge is the right of every human being, and participation in its generation, application and diffusion a responsibility that all must shoulder in the great enterprise of building a prosperous world civilization—each individual according to his or her talents and abilities." This orientation has particularly manifested itself in the Bahá'í community's focus on education, which has been a central concern since the inception of the Faith; in its efforts to foster in individuals a growing consciousness and capacity to recognize prejudice and to counter it; in its practice of using consultative processes in all its affairs; and in its commitment to and upholding of the dual knowledge systems of science and religion as being necessary for the advancement of civilization. Moreover, the development of the life of the mind and independent investigation of reality, which are highly prized in the Bahá'í writings, serve to equip individuals to distinguish truth from falsehood, which is so essential if prejudices, superstitious beliefs, and outworn traditions that impede unity are to be eliminated. 'Abdu'l-Bahá offers the assurance in this respect that "once every soul inquireth into truth, society will be freed from the darkness of continually repeating the past."

(From a letter dated 27 December 2017 written on behalf of the Universal House of Justice to an individual believer)   [63]

THE NATURE OF BAHÁ'Í SOCIAL AND ECONOMIC DEVELOPMENT

Coherence between the Material and Spiritual Dimensions of Existence

. . . whatever is in the heavens and whatever is on the earth is a direct evidence of the revelation within it of the attributes and names of God, inasmuch as within every atom are enshrined the signs that bear eloquent testimony to the revelation of that most great Light.

(Bahá'u'lláh, The Kitáb-i-Íqán, ¶107)   [64]

Religion is verily the chief instrument for the establishment of order in the world and of tranquility amongst its peoples. . . . The greater the decline of religion, the more grievous the waywardness of the ungodly. This cannot but lead in the end to chaos and confusion.

(Bahá'u'lláh, *Tablets of Bahá'u'lláh Revealed after the Kitáb-i-Aqdas,* pp. 63–64)   [65]

. . . religion must be in conformity with science and reason, so that it may influence the hearts of men. The foundation must be solid and must not consist of imitations.

('Abdu'l-Bahá, First Tablet to The Hague)   [66]

. . . although material civilization is one of the means for the progress of the world of mankind, yet until it becomes combined with Divine civilization, the desired result, which is the felicity of mankind, will

33

not be attained. . . . Material civilization is like a lamp-glass. Divine civilization is the lamp itself and the glass without the light is dark. Material civilization is like the body. No matter how infinitely graceful, elegant and beautiful it may be, it is dead. Divine civilization is like the spirit, and the body gets its life from the spirit, otherwise it becomes a corpse. It has thus been made evident that the world of mankind is in need of the breaths of the Holy Spirit. Without the spirit the world of mankind is lifeless, and without this light the world of mankind is in utter darkness.

('Abdu'l-Bahá, First Tablet to The Hague) [67]

. . . until material achievements, physical accomplishments and human virtues are reinforced by spiritual perfections, luminous qualities and characteristics of mercy, no fruit or result shall issue therefrom, nor will the happiness of the world of humanity, which is the ultimate aim, be attained. For although, on the one hand, material achievements and the development of the physical world produce prosperity, which exquisitely manifests its intended aims, on the other hand dangers, severe calamities and violent afflictions are imminent.

('Abdu'l-Bahá, *Selections from the Writings of 'Abdu'l-Bahá*, no. 225.5) [68]

We hope that the beloved of God and the handmaids of the Merciful will, in accordance with the heavenly Teachings, serve the oneness of the world of humanity, regard religion as the basis of love and fellowship amongst the people, strive to harmonize religion and science, become a treasury of riches for the poor and a shelter and asylum for the fugitive, bring joy and radiance to the destitute, and aid the needy through the strengthening grace of the All-Merciful.

('Abdu'l-Bahá, from a Tablet—translated from the Persian) [69]

Material civilization is like unto the lamp, while spiritual civilization is the light in that lamp. If the material and spiritual civilization become united, then we will have the light and the lamp together, and the outcome will be perfect. For material civilization is like unto a beautiful body, and spiritual civilization is like unto the spirit of life. If that wondrous spirit of life enters this beautiful body, the body will become a channel for the distribution and development of the perfections of humanity.

('Abdu'l-Bahá, *The Promulgation of Universal Peace*, p. 15) [70]

For man two wings are necessary. One wing is physical power and material civilization; the other is spiritual power and divine civilization. With one wing only, flight is impossible. Two wings are essential. Therefore, no matter how much material civilization advances, it cannot attain to perfection except through the uplift of spiritual civilization.

('Abdu'l-Bahá, *The Promulgation of Universal Peace*, p. 16) [71]

No matter how far the material world advances, it cannot establish the happiness of mankind. Only when material and spiritual civilization are linked and coordinated will happiness be assured. Then material civilization will not contribute its energies to the forces of evil in destroying the oneness of humanity, for in material civilization good and evil advance together and maintain the same pace. For example, consider the material progress of man in the last decade. Schools and colleges, hospitals, philanthropic institutions, scientific academies and temples of philosophy have been founded, but hand in hand with these evidences of development, the invention and production of means and weapons for human destruction have correspondingly increased. . . .

All this is the outcome of material civilization; therefore, although material advancement furthers good purposes in life, at the same time it serves evil ends. . . . If the moral precepts and foundations of divine civilization become united with the material advancement of man, there is no doubt that the happiness of the human world will be attained and that from every direction the glad tidings of peace upon earth will be announced. Then humankind will achieve extraordinary progress, the sphere of human intelligence will be immeasurably enlarged, wonderful inventions will appear, and the spirit of God will reveal itself; all men will consort in joy and fragrance, and eternal life will be conferred upon the children of the Kingdom. . . . Therefore, the material and the divine, or merciful, civilizations must progress together until the highest aspirations and desires of humanity shall become realized.

('Abdu'l-Bahá, *The Promulgation of Universal Peace*, pp. 151–52) [72]

Scientific knowledge is the highest attainment upon the human plane, for science is the discoverer of realities. It is of two kinds: material and spiritual. Material science is the investigation of natural phenomena; divine science is the discovery and realization of spiritual verities. The world of humanity must acquire both. A bird has two wings; it cannot fly with one. Material and spiritual science are the two wings of human uplift and attainment. Both are necessary—one the natural, the other supernatural; one material, the other divine.

('Abdu'l-Bahá, *The Promulgation of Universal Peace*, pp. 195–96) [73]

God has endowed man with intelligence and reason whereby he is required to determine the verity of questions and propositions. If religious beliefs and opinions are found contrary to the standards of science, they are mere superstitions and imaginations; for the antithesis of knowledge is ignorance, and the child of ignorance is superstition. Unquestionably there must be agreement between true religion and science. If a question be found contrary to reason, faith and belief in it are impossible, and there is no outcome but wavering and vacillation.

(ʿAbduʾl-Bahá, *The Promulgation of Universal Peace*, pp. 251–52) [74]

No matter how much the world of humanity advances in material civilization, it is nevertheless in need of the spiritual development mentioned in the Gospel. The virtues of the material world are limited, whereas divine virtues are unlimited. Inasmuch as material virtues are limited, man's need of the perfections of the divine world is unlimited.

Throughout human history we find that although the very apex of human virtues has been reached at various times, yet they were limited, whereas divine attainments have ever been unbounded and infinite. The limited is ever in need of the unlimited. The material must be correlated with the spiritual. The material may be likened to the body, but divine virtues are the breathings of the Holy Spirit itself. The body without spirit is not capable of real accomplishment. Although it may be in the utmost condition of beauty and excellence, it is, nevertheless, in need of the spirit. The chimney of the lamp, no matter how polished and perfect it be, is in need of the light. Without the light, the lamp or candle is not illuminating. Without the spirit, the body is not productive.

(ʿAbduʾl-Bahá, *The Promulgation of Universal Peace*, p. 287) [75]

This last world war together with the treaty of peace and its consequences have taught humanity that unless national, religious and political prejudices be abolished, unless universal brotherhood be established, unless spiritual civilization be given an equal footing with material civilization and thereby change the standard of individual, national and international morality, the world is doomed to failure and society to utter destruction.

(From a letter written circa 1924 on behalf of Shoghi Effendi to an individual believer) [76]

The present social and economic problems that are facing the British people are surely occupying their whole attention, but they should also operate as a reminder and draw them closer to spiritual matters. The people have to be made conscious of the fact that without a complete change in our outlook and a total reform of the guiding principles of our life, such as the Cause advocates, our social and economic problems cannot be solved nor our conditions ameliorated.

(From a letter dated 7 November 1931 written on behalf of Shoghi Effendi to an individual believer) [77]

It is not merely material well-being that people need. What they desperately need is to know how to live their lives—they need to know who they are, to what purpose they exist, and how they should act towards one another; and, once they know the answers to these questions they need to be helped to gradually apply these answers to everyday behaviour. It is to the solution of this basic problem of mankind that the greater part of all our energy and resources should be directed.
. . .

. . . we know that the working of the material world is merely a reflection of spiritual conditions and until the spiritual conditions can be changed there can be no lasting change for the better in material affairs.

(The Universal House of Justice, from a message dated 19 November 1974 to a National Spiritual Assembly) [78]

With regard to the harmony of science and religion, the Writings of the Central Figures and the commentaries of the Guardian make abundantly clear that the task of humanity, including the Bahá'í community that serves as the "leaven" within it, is to create a global civilization which embodies both the spiritual and material dimensions of existence. The nature and scope of such a civilization are still beyond anything the present generation can conceive. The prosecution of this vast enterprise will depend on a progressive interaction between the truths and principles of religion and the discoveries and insights of scientific inquiry. This entails living with ambiguities as a natural and inescapable feature of the process of exploring reality. It also requires us not to limit science to any particular school of thought or methodological approach postulated in the course of its development. The challenge facing Bahá'í thinkers is to provide responsible leadership in this endeavour, since it is they who have both the priceless insights of the Revelation and the advantages conferred by scientific investigation.

(From a letter dated 19 May 1995 written on behalf of the Universal House of Justice to an individual believer)   [79]

. . . religion and science are the two indispensable knowledge systems through which the potentialities of consciousness develop. Far from being in conflict with one another, these fundamental modes of the mind's exploration of reality are mutually dependent and have been most productive in those rare but happy periods of history when their complementary nature has been recognized and they have been able to work together. The insights and skills generated by scientific advance will have always to look to the guidance of spiritual and moral commitment to ensure their appropriate application; religious convictions, no matter how cherished they

may be, must submit, willingly and gratefully, to impartial testing
by scientific methods.

> (The Universal House of Justice, from a message dated April
> 2002 to the World's Religious Leaders) [80]

. . . science and religion are two complementary systems of knowledge and practice by which human beings come to understand the world
around them and through which civilization advances; . . . religion
without science soon degenerates into superstition and fanaticism, while
science without religion becomes the tool of crude materialism; . . . true
prosperity, the fruit of a dynamic coherence between the material and
spiritual requirements of life, will recede further and further out of reach
as long as consumerism continues to act as opium to the human soul. . . .

> (The Universal House of Justice, from a message dated 2 March
> 2013 to the Bahá'ís of Iran) [81]

As the place from which spiritual forces are to radiate, the
Mashriqu'l-Adhkár is the focal point for dependencies to be raised up
for the well-being of humanity and is the expression of a common will
and eagerness to serve. These dependencies—centres of education and
scientific learning as well as cultural and humanitarian endeavour—
embody the ideals of social and spiritual progress to be achieved through
the application of knowledge, and demonstrate how, when religion and
science are in harmony, they elevate the station of the human being and
lead to the flourishing of civilization. As your lives amply demonstrate,
worship, though essential to the inner life of the human being and vital to
spiritual development, must also lead to deeds that give outward expression to that inner transformation. This concept of worship—inseparable
from service—is promulgated by the Mashriqu'l-Adhkár.

> (The Universal House of Justice, from a message dated
> 18 December 2014 to the Bahá'ís in Iran) [82]

Capacity Building, Participation, and Organic Growth

We must now highly resolve to arise and lay hold of all those instrumentalities that promote the peace and well-being and happiness, the knowledge, culture and industry, the dignity, value and station, of the entire human race. Thus, through the restoring waters of pure intention and unselfish effort, the earth of human potentialities will blossom with its own latent excellence and flower into praiseworthy qualities, and bear and flourish until it comes to rival that rosegarden of knowledge which belonged to our forefathers.

('Abdu'l-Bahá, *The Secret of Divine Civilization*, ¶8)   [83]

The world of politics is like the world of man; he is seed at first, and then passes by degrees to the condition of embryo and foetus, acquiring a bone structure, being clothed with flesh, taking on his own special form, until at last he reaches the plane where he can befittingly fulfill the words: "the most excellent of Makers." Just as this is a requirement of creation and is based on the universal Wisdom, the political world in the same way cannot instantaneously evolve from the nadir of defectiveness to the zenith of rightness and perfection. Rather, qualified individuals must strive by day and by night, using all those means which will conduce to progress, until the government and the people develop along every line from day to day and even from moment to moment.

('Abdu'l-Bahá, *The Secret of Divine Civilization*, ¶190)   [84]

In all the prophetic Dispensations, philanthropic affairs were confined to their respective peoples only—with the exception of small matters, such as charity, which it was permissible to extend to others. But in this wonderful Dispensation, philanthropic undertakings are for all humanity, without any exception, because this is the manifestation of the mercifulness of God.

('Abdu'l-Bahá, from a talk—translated from the Persian)   [85]

It is even as the seed: The tree exists within it but is hidden and concealed; when the seed grows and develops, the tree appears in its fullness. In like manner, the growth and development of all beings proceeds by gradual degrees. This is the universal and divinely ordained law and the natural order. The seed does not suddenly become the tree; the embryo does not at once become the man; the mineral substance does not in a moment become the stone: No, all these grow and develop gradually until they attain the limit of perfection.

('Abdu'l-Bahá, *Some Answered Questions*, no. 51.3)   [86]

In a living organism the full measure of its development is not known or realized at the time of its inception or birth. Development and progression imply gradual stages or degrees. For example, spiritual advancement may be likened to the light of the early dawn. Although this dawn light is dim and pale, a wise man who views the march of the sunrise at its very beginning can foretell the ascendancy of the sun in its full glory and effulgence. He knows for a certainty that it is the beginning of its manifestation and that later it will assume great power and potency. Again, for example, if he takes a seed and observes that it is sprouting, he will know assuredly that it will ultimately become a tree.

('Abdu'l-Bahá, *The Promulgation of Universal Peace*, pp. 181–82)   [87]

The realities of things have been revealed in this radiant century, and that which is true must come to the surface. Among these realities is the principle of the equality of man and woman—equal rights and prerogatives in all things appertaining to humanity. . . . Woman must especially devote her energies and abilities toward the industrial and agricultural sciences, seeking to assist mankind in that which is most needful. By this means she will demonstrate capability and ensure recognition of equality in the social and economic equation.

('Abdu'l-Bahá, *The Promulgation of Universal Peace*, p. 395)[88]

Another essential requirement is the expediting of the tasks of transcribing, collecting and despatching the Sacred Writings to the Holy Land, and recording the general history of the Cause of God. The Western believers in the far-flung reaches of the free world, who have set about prosecuting important plans, are anxious and expectant that these two tasks be speedily completed and the necessary preparations for their forthcoming projects be made without delay, thus enabling them to give concrete expression to their hopes and plans for the future, and to impart a great momentum to the spread of the Holy Cause.

The same applies to the participation of the friends in charitable, scientific, and literary associations. The friends must, with wisdom and moderation, after careful consultation, and according to their capacity and means, assist any association that sincerely aims to contribute to the common weal and to the best interests of the world of humanity. They should participate to the extent possible, but must refrain from the least involvement in politics, whether in their deeds, hearts, or words, and must shun and avoid any association with malevolent and contending parties.

(Shoghi Effendi, from a letter dated September 1926 written to the Bahá'ís of the East—translated from the Persian)   [89]

We cannot segregate the human heart from the environment outside us and say that once one of these is reformed everything will be improved. Man is organic with the world. His inner life moulds the environment and is itself also deeply affected by it. The one acts upon the other and every abiding change in the life of man is the result of these mutual reactions.

(From a letter dated 17 February 1933 written on behalf of Shoghi Effendi to an individual believer) [90]

"Regard the world as the human body," wrote Bahá'u'lláh to Queen Victoria. . . . In the human body, every cell, every organ, every nerve has its part to play. When all do so the body is healthy, vigorous, radiant, ready for every call made upon it. No cell, however humble, lives apart from the body, whether in serving it or receiving from it. This is true of the body of mankind in which God has "endowed each and all with talents and faculties," and is supremely true of the body of the Bahá'í world community, for this body is already an organism, united in its aspirations, unified in its methods, seeking assistance and confirmation from the same Source, and illumined with the conscious knowledge of its unity. Therefore, in this organic, divinely guided, blessed, and illumined body the participation of every believer is of the utmost importance, and is a source of power and vitality as yet unknown to us. . . .

The real secret of universal participation lies in the Master's oft expressed wish that the friends should love each other, constantly encourage each other, work together, be as one soul in one body, and in so doing become a true, organic, healthy body animated and illumined by the spirit. In such a body all will receive spiritual health and vitality from the organism itself, and the most perfect flowers and fruits will be brought forth.

(The Universal House of Justice, from a message dated September 1964 to the Bahá'ís of the World) [91]

As you can see, all these developments relate directly to the teaching work inasmuch as the Bahá'í communities must reach a certain size before they can begin to implement many of them. How, for example, can a Bahá'í community demonstrate effectively the abolition of prejudices which divide the inhabitants of a country until it has a cross-section of those inhabitants within its ranks? A seed is the vital origin of a tree and of a tremendous importance for that reason, but it cannot produce fruit until it has grown into a tree and flowered and fruited. So a Bahá'í community of nine believers is a vital step, since it can bring into being for that locality the divine institution of the Local Spiritual Assembly, but it is still only a seed, and needs to grow in size and in the diversity of its members before it can produce really convincing fruit for its fellow-citizens.

(From a letter dated 3 January 1982 written on behalf of the Universal House of Justice to an individual believer)   [92]

There are two principles which the House of Justice feels are fundamental to the generality of such projects of social and economic development, although, of course, there will be exceptions. The first is that they should be built on a substructure of existing, sufficiently strong local Bahá'í communities. The second is that the long-term conduct of the project should aim at self-sufficiency and not be dependent upon continuing financial support from outside.

The first principle implies that the projects of social and economic development now to be undertaken are a natural stage of the growth of the Bahá'í community and are needed by the community itself, although they will, of course, benefit a much wider segment of society. . . .

The second principle must take into account that any project started by the Cause should be designed to grow soundly and steadily, and not to collapse from attrition. In other words, external assistance and funds, Bahá'í and non-Bahá'í, may be used for capital acquisitions, to make surveys, to initiate activities, to bring in expertise, but the aim should be for each project to be able to continue and to develop on the strength of local Bahá'í labour, funds and enthusiasm even if all external aid should be cut off.

(From a letter dated 8 May 1984 written on behalf of the Universal House of Justice to a National Spiritual Assembly) [93]

The second fundamental principle[2] which enables us to understand the pattern towards which Bahá'u'lláh wishes human society to evolve is the principle of organic growth which requires that detailed developments, and the understanding of detailed developments, become available only with the passage of time and with the help of the guidance given by that Central Authority in the Cause to whom all must turn. In this regard one can use the simile of a tree. If a farmer plants a tree, he cannot state at that moment what its exact height will be, the number of its branches or the exact time of its blossoming. He can, however, give a general impression of its size and pattern of growth and can state with confidence which fruit it will bear. The same is true of the evolution of the World Order of Bahá'u'lláh.

(From a letter dated 27 April 1995 written on behalf of the Universal House of Justice to an individual believer) [94]

---

2. The first principle referred to in this letter is "the principle that the writings of 'Abdu'l-Bahá and the Guardian are thoroughly imbued with the spirit of the Revelation of Bahá'u'lláh and intimately linked with the Teachings of Bahá'u'lláh Himself." See *Messages from the Universal House of Justice, 1986–2001, the Fourth Epoch of the Formative Age* (Wilmette: Bahá'í Publishing, 2009), no. 201.9–11.

These projects include schools, literacy programmes, moral education classes, academic training, health plans, special programmes for the advancement of women and minority groups, agricultural programmes, and special programmes for the conservation of the environment, etc. Experience has shown that if help is provided from abroad without the cooperation and involvement of the local inhabitants, the locals do not consider the project as something that belongs to them and feel no responsibility toward it, but if they initiate the process of identifying their needs and take part in the decision-making and execution processes they will feel responsible for the preservation and continued operation of the project.

(From a letter dated 30 July 1996 written on behalf of the Universal House of Justice to an individual believer) [95]

The worldwide Bahá'í community, as an organic whole, transcends divisions prevalent in society today, such as "North" and "South," "developed" and "underdeveloped." Social and economic development efforts are undertaken by Bahá'ís, irrespective of the degree of material prosperity achieved by their nations, as they strive to apply the teachings of Bahá'u'lláh to the gradual process of building a new civilization. Every follower of Bahá'u'lláh is a member of this worldwide community and can rightfully offer to contribute to a specific endeavor in any country. As the friends gain experience in social and economic development, and as they advance in their studies of various branches of learning or in their professional fields, individuals arise in every continent who have expertise in some aspect of development work and who wish to offer their services to projects at home or abroad. If their energies are not channelled effectively, and they are not given a realistic picture of Bahá'í development efforts, these friends will later become frustrated when they realize that the capacity of Bahá'í projects overseas to utilize their talents and services is limited.

For this reason, it is important that conferences, seminars and promotional materials not reinforce an image of "development projects" as understood by society at large. Bahá'í efforts in this field generally take the form of grassroots initiatives carried out by small groups of believers in the towns and villages where they reside. As these initiatives are nurtured, some grow into more substantial programs with permanent administrative structures. Yet very few can be compared with the kind of complex projects promoted and funded by government agencies and large nongovernmental organizations.

The effective use of the talents of individuals with particular expertise also demands vigilance in ensuring that the initiative of some, usually those with access to more resources, does not end up suffocating the initiatives of others. The Administrative Order is structured in a way that fosters initiative and safeguards the right of people to be meaningfully involved in the development of their own communities. Accordingly the activities of the friends in each country fall under the guidance of the institutions of the Faith in that country. . . .

In general, the determining factor in matching offers of service and assistance to projects should be the capacity of the projects to receive help and not the amount of resources available. It is quite possible that the talents of the friends, especially those in . . . exceed the capacity of the development projects elsewhere to receive assistance at this stage in the growth of the Faith. In this connection, the two-pronged approach you are pursuing seems most appropriate. While striving to help increase the capacity of projects worldwide, you are at the same time encouraging individual believers from more materially prosperous countries to become involved in Bahá'í projects at home. You should also continue encouraging them to participate in worthy endeavors outside the Faith in order to influence their professional fields and infuse them with the teachings of Bahá'u'lláh. They should be assured that this is, in and of itself, a tremendous service to the Cause and not feel that they are serving the Faith only if they dedicate themselves directly to Bahá'í projects.

(The Universal House of Justice, from a memorandum dated 11 March 1997 to the Office of Social and Economic Development) [96]

Humanity's crying need will not be met by a struggle among competing ambitions or by protest against one or another of the countless wrongs afflicting a desperate age. It calls, rather, for a fundamental change of consciousness, for a wholehearted embrace of Bahá'u'lláh's teaching that the time has come when each human being on earth must learn to accept responsibility for the welfare of the entire human family.

(The Universal House of Justice, from a message dated 24 May 2001 to the Believers Gathered for the Events Marking the Completion of the Projects on Mount Carmel) [97]

As you know, the attention of the Bahá'í world has been, and will continue to be for at least the next fifteen years, focused on advancing the process of entry by troops. It is expected that, as this process gathers momentum at the local level, one of the natural consequences will be the emergence of a vibrant Bahá'í community life characterized by a desire to apply the teachings of Bahá'u'lláh to the needs of society. Effective social action will result, then, as capacity at the grassroots of the community increases and collective consciousness is raised.

(From a letter dated 6 September 2006 written on behalf of the Universal House of Justice to an individual believer) [98]

A greater involvement in the life of society, individually and collectively, will be an inevitable outcome as the process of growth gathers momentum in advanced clusters. In Bahá'í communities with limited resources too much involvement in such efforts at an early stage may dissipate their energies and detract from the coherence of activities necessary for growth. Yet, in areas where the Faith has sufficiently consolidated itself, it is natural to expect that Bahá'ís would engage in social action, initially by finding ways to apply the Teachings to the problems afflicting their families, neighbors and the communities in which they live.

(From a letter dated 11 September 2008 written on behalf of the Universal House of Justice to an individual believer)   [99]

In its Riḍván 2008 message, the House of Justice observed that, as the work of expansion and consolidation progresses, Bahá'ís will be drawn further and further into the life of the society around them. The nature of this encounter will necessarily be organic, gradual, and guided by the learning process in which the believers everywhere are already engaged. Moreover, it is hoped that the Bahá'í community's increasing involvement with society will occur naturally in every cluster around the world.

(From a letter dated 16 June 2009 written on behalf of the Universal House of Justice to an individual believer)   [100]

. . . every human being and every group of individuals, irrespective of whether they are counted among His followers, can take inspiration from His teachings, benefiting from whatever gems of wisdom and knowledge will aid them in addressing the challenges they face. Indeed, the civilization that beckons humanity will not be attained through the efforts of the Bahá'í community alone. Numerous groups and organizations, animated by the spirit of world solidarity that is an indirect manifestation of Bahá'u'lláh's conception of the principle of

the oneness of humankind, will contribute to the civilization destined
to emerge out of the welter and chaos of present-day society.

(The Universal House of Justice, Riḍván 2010 message to the
Bahá'ís of the World) [101]

As noted in the Riḍván message, social change is not a project that
one group of people carries out for the benefit of another. The scope
and complexity of social action, the message explains, must be commensurate with the human resources available in a village or neighbourhood to carry it forward. This implies that efforts best begin on a
modest scale and grow organically as capacity within the population
develops—essentially capacity to apply with increasing effectiveness
elements of Bahá'u'lláh's Revelation, together with the contents and
methods of science, to social reality. In this light, the House of Justice has made clear in many of its recent messages that, at the present
stage in the development of the Faith, building capacity to address the
material needs of a local community should not be considered in isolation from a process already set in motion to address its spiritual needs.
This process, of course, gathers momentum as devotional meetings,
children's classes, junior youth groups and study circles are established
in a region. It is directed by the institutions and agencies of the Faith
and depends heavily on the exercise of initiative by a growing number of individuals in the region concerned for the well-being of their
communities. It is such individuals—men and women, young and
old—who, thus empowered, begin to make and implement decisions
about their spiritual and material progress, increasing still further their
collective capacity as they do so. Depending on the circumstances in
the region, the endeavours of a non-profit development organization,
operating in keeping with the principles of the Faith, may well help to

facilitate this now more complex process of empowerment unfolding in the region. Such an organization, which itself emerges organically and grows in strength over time, functions under the moral guidance of the institutions in the country. Those most intimately involved with the organization by necessity submit themselves to the discipline needed to ensure that their efforts constantly serve to contribute to the empowerment of a population, requiring them to work close to the grassroots, alongside the people themselves; to share in their struggles; and to recognize that economic benefits will be few.

(From a letter dated 18 July 2010 written on behalf of the Universal House of Justice to an individual believer)   [102]

A small community, whose members are united by their shared beliefs, characterized by their high ideals, proficient in managing their affairs and tending to their needs, and perhaps engaged in several humanitarian projects—a community such as this, prospering but at a comfortable distance from the reality experienced by the masses of humanity, can never hope to serve as a pattern for restructuring the whole of society. That the worldwide Bahá'í community has managed to avert the dangers of complacency is a source of abiding joy to us. Indeed, the community has well in hand its expansion and consolidation. Yet, to administer the affairs of teeming numbers in villages and cities around the globe—to raise aloft the standard of Bahá'u'lláh's World Order for all to see—is still a distant goal.

Therein, then, lies the challenge that must be faced by those in the forefront of the learning process which will continue to advance over the course of the next Plan. Wherever an intensive programme of growth is established, let the friends spare no effort to increase the level of participation. Let them strain every nerve to ensure that the system which they have so laboriously erected does not close in on itself but progressively expands to embrace more and more people. . . . And let them not forget the lessons of the past which left no doubt that a relatively small band of active supporters of the Cause, no matter how resourceful, no matter how consecrated, cannot attend to the needs of communities comprising hundreds, much less thousands, of men, women and children.

(The Universal House of Justice, from a message dated 28 December 2010 to the Conference of the Continental Boards of Counsellors) [103]

The pattern of spiritual and social life taking shape in clusters that involves study circles, children's classes, junior youth groups, devotional meetings, home visits, teaching efforts, and reflection meetings, as well as Holy Day observances, Nineteen Day Feasts, and other gatherings, provides abundant opportunities for engagement, experience, consultation, and learning that will lead to change in personal and collective understanding and action. Issues of prejudice of race, class, and color will inevitably arise as the friends reach out to diverse populations, especially in the closely knit context of neighborhoods. There, every activity can take a form most suited to the culture and interests of the population, so that new believers can be quickened and confirmed in a nurturing and familiar environment, until they are able to offer their share to the resolution of the challenges faced by a growing Bahá'í community. For this is not a process that some carry out on behalf of others who are passive recipients—the mere extension of a congregation and invitation to paternalism—but one in which an ever-increasing number of souls recognize and take responsibility for the transformation of humanity set in motion by Bahá'u'lláh. In an environment of love and trust born of common belief, practice, and mission, individuals of different races will have the intimate connection of heart and mind upon which mutual understanding and change depend. As a result of their training and deepening, a growing number of believers will draw insights from the Writings to sensitively and effectively address issues of racial prejudice that arise within their personal lives and families, among community members, and in social settings and the workplace. As programs of growth advance and the scope and intensity of activities grow, the friends will be drawn into participation in conversations and, in time, initiatives for social action at the grassroots where issues pertaining to freedom from prejudice naturally emerge, whether directly or indirectly.

(From a letter dated 10 April 2011 written on behalf of the Universal House of Justice to an individual believer) [104]

You will no doubt be familiar with the guidance provided by the Universal House of Justice in its Riḍván 2010 message concerning "certain fundamental concepts" that pertain to instances of social action pursued by Baháʼís, which would include social and economic development projects. Among these are the principles that "while social action may involve the provision of goods and services in some form, its primary concern must be to build capacity within a given population to participate in creating a better world" and that "social change is not a project that one group of people carries out for the benefit of another." Indeed, such endeavours are best initiated from within the communities they are intended to benefit, and great care must be exercised so as to ensure that the resources available from outside the community do not define the nature of the projects undertaken. In places around the world where the process of growth is advancing well, the enhanced capabilities fostered within individuals by the training institute process are naturally giving rise to sustainable programmes of social action at the grassroots, as it is the members of a given community who are in the best position to understand their social reality, assess their needs, and trace their own path of progress. For this reason, Baháʼís are discouraged from designing and implementing development projects in countries other than their own.

(From a letter dated 22 October 2012 written on behalf of the Universal House of Justice to an individual believer)   [105]

What should be stated plainly here is that Bahá'ís do not believe the transformation thus envisioned will come about exclusively through their own efforts. Nor are they trying to create a movement that would seek to impose on society their vision of the future. Every nation and every group—indeed, every individual—will, to a greater or lesser degree, contribute to the emergence of the world civilization towards which humanity is irresistibly moving.

(The Universal House of Justice, from a message dated 2 March 2013 to the Bahá'ís of Iran)   [106]

At the heart of such an approach lies the question of capacity building. It has been observed in cluster after cluster that the capacity to carry out efforts in the area of social action is gradually raised as growing numbers of individuals are involved in the institute process and are assisted to dedicate their energies to the spiritual and material transformation of the regions in which they live. Generally speaking, Bahá'í social and economic development efforts begin at the grassroots, start small, and grow organically, commensurate with the local human and financial resources available to them. In this connection, as noted in the Riḍván message of 2010, social change should not be conceived of as a project that one group of people carries out for the benefit of another, nor should it be reduced to the mere delivery of goods or services. In light of these considerations, Bahá'ís are discouraged from implementing projects in countries where they do not reside. Further, for a number of reasons, considerable caution needs to be exercised in cases where external funds are made available to a particular endeavor. Experience has shown, for example, that the right of the local community to trace its own path of progress can be compromised when those providing resources from outside of the community assume responsibility for the management and direction of an initiative or exert undue influence on the nature of projects undertaken. Moreover, organizations which are solely reliant on external support often struggle to sustain their activities in the event that outside sources of funding are withdrawn. In order to avoid such challenges, the Office of Social and Economic Development at the Bahá'í World Centre helps to coordinate the flow of resources to Bahá'í-inspired development projects, taking into account both the conditions in the region and the maturity of particular initiatives.

(From a letter dated 19 April 2013 written on behalf of the Universal House of Justice to an individual believer)   [107]

. . . development, from a Bahá'í perspective, is viewed as a process, the main protagonists of which are the people themselves. Emphasis is placed on building the capacity of communities to make and implement decisions about their spiritual and material progress. This necessitates a process whereby small-scale endeavors emerge organically from a pattern of community life which is created as the friends in a given cluster gain experience in applying the framework for action associated with the Five Year Plan. As the believers engage in the processes of expansion and consolidation, they acquire through their efforts a sharper understanding of the challenges faced by the populations they serve and gradually learn to apply the Teachings of the Faith to the pressing needs of their communities. Experience throughout the Bahá'í world has demonstrated that it is generally unproductive to introduce external agencies, technologies, or funding sources at an early stage—that is, before capacity to initiate and sustain projects is built at the grassroots.

(From a letter dated 30 December 2014 written on behalf of the Universal House of Justice to an individual believer)   [108]

In its early stages, the systematic effort to reach out to a population and foster its participation in the process of capacity building accelerates markedly when members of that population are themselves in the vanguard of such an effort. These individuals will have special insight into those forces and structures in their societies that can, in various ways, reinforce the endeavours under way.

(The Universal House of Justice, from a message dated 29 December 2015 to the Conference of the Continental Boards of Counsellors)   [109]

. . . Bahá'ís are engaged in cities and villages across the globe in establishing a pattern of life in which increasing numbers, irrespective of background, are invited to take part. This pattern, expressive of the dynamic coherence between the material and spiritual dimensions of life, includes classes for the spiritual education of children in which they also develop a deep appreciation for the fundamental unity of the various world religions; groups that assist young people to navigate a crucial stage of their lives and to withstand the corrosive forces that especially target them; circles of study wherein participants reflect on the spiritual nature of existence and build capacity for service to the community and society; gatherings for collective worship that strengthen the devotional character of the community; and, in time, a growing range of endeavours for social and economic development. This pattern of community life is giving rise to vibrant and purposeful new communities wherein relationships are founded on the oneness of mankind, universal participation, justice, and freedom from prejudice. All are welcome. The process which is unfolding seeks to foster collaboration and build capacity within every human group—with no regard to class or religious background, with no concern for ethnicity or race, and irrespective of gender or social status—to arise and contribute to the advancement of civilization.

(From a letter dated 27 December 2017 written on behalf of the Universal House of Justice to an individual believer)   [110]

The Emergence of Social Action

He has noted with keen interest the plan you have conceived for the intensification of agricultural production with the view of meeting any possible food shortage in these times of war. While he is fully aware of the need for putting forth such a plan, and deeply appreciative as he feels of the noble motives that have prompted you to approach this problem, he nevertheless thinks that the time is not yet ripe for the believers, as a body, to undertake social and economic experiments of such character and scope. Neither the material resources at their disposal, nor their numerical strength are sufficient to give them any reasonable hope of embarking successfully upon a project of this kind.

(From a letter dated 6 November 1940 written on behalf of Shoghi Effendi to an individual believer)   [111]

Now is not the time for the friends to seek to establish a Bahá'í village; they have definite tasks confronting them of the utmost importance and urgency, and on these they should concentrate their attention. Nor does the Guardian feel it is necessary for the friends to buy land at this time. In the future, when they have accomplished the goals set out for them by the beloved Master Himself, they will be able to develop more community projects, but now such enterprises would merely dissipate their strength, which should all be directed into the teaching work.

(From a letter dated 26 March 1943 written on behalf of Shoghi Effendi to an individual believer)   [112]

The believers must not take their eyes off their own immediate tasks of patiently consolidating their administrative institutions, building up new Assemblies . . . and labouring to perfect the Bahá'í pattern of life, for these are things that no other group of people in the world can do or will do, and they alone are able to provide the spiritual foundation and example on which the larger world schemes must ultimately rest. At the same time every effort should be made to broadcast the Teachings at this time, and correlate them to the plight of humanity and the plans for its future.

(From a letter dated 29 March 1945 written on behalf of Shoghi Effendi to a National Spiritual Assembly)   [113]

A wider horizon is opening before us, illumined by a growing and universal manifestation of the inherent potentialities of the Cause for ordering human affairs. In this light can be discerned not only our immediate tasks but, more dimly, new pursuits and undertakings upon which we must shortly become engaged. . . .

. . . The powers released by Bahá'u'lláh match the needs of the times. We may therefore be utterly confident that the new throb of energy now vibrating throughout the Cause will empower it to meet the oncoming challenges of assisting, as maturity and resources allow, the development of the social and economic life of peoples, of collaborating with the forces leading towards the establishment of order in the world, of influencing the exploitation and constructive uses of modern technology, and in all these ways enhancing the prestige and progress of the Faith and uplifting the conditions of the generality of mankind.

(The Universal House of Justice, Riḍván 140 (1983) message to the Bahá'ís of the World) [114]

The message of the House of Justice dated 20 October 1983 has clearly set out the concepts, defined the objectives and outlined the guiding principles for the selection and implementation of Bahá'í development projects, programmes or activities. The vast majority of Bahá'í projects will be primarily generated at the grass roots, and, initially as required, will receive help from Bahá'í sources, in terms of finances and manpower. The projects will, as you have already surmised, be non-profit making, concerned mainly with activities closely related to education, health and hygiene, agriculture and simple community development activities. It is hoped that all these types of projects will reflect the strength of the spiritual principles enshrined in the Teachings of Bahá'u'lláh.

It is important that our undertakings be modest in their scope at the present time. Then, as we gain in confidence and experience and as our resources increase, our work will encompass expanded objectives, and the friends will explore new areas of social and economic activity.

(From a letter dated 22 December 1983 written on behalf of the Universal House of Justice to an individual believer) [115]

The relationship between teaching and social and economic development needs to be considered both in terms of certain fundamental principles and in the context of the processes which characterize the growth of the Bahá'í community. You are well aware of the relevant principles, which include the following: Bahá'ís should give the teachings of Bahá'u'lláh liberally and unconditionally to humanity so that people may apply them to pressing social issues and uplift themselves materially and spiritually; in their dealings with society at large, the friends should be upright and avoid any trace of deception; social and economic development projects should not be used as an inducement to conversion; and funds from non-Bahá'ís should not be utilized for strictly Bahá'í purposes. None of these diminishes the importance of the sacred obligation to teach the Cause. Teaching should remain the dominating passion of the life of every individual believer, and growth a major concern of the Bahá'í community.

As the Bahá'í community has moved from one stage to the next, the range of activities that it has been able to undertake has increased. Its growth has been organic in nature and has implied gradual differentiation in functions. When the Bahá'í community was small in size, all of its interactions with society at large easily fitted together under the designation of direct and indirect teaching. But, over time, new dimensions of work appeared—involvement in civil society, highly organized diplomatic work, social action, and so on—each with its own aims, methods and resources. In a certain sense, it is possible to refer to all of these activities as teaching, since their ultimate purpose is the diffusion of the divine fragrances, the offering of Bahá'u'lláh's Revelation to humankind, and service to society. But, in practice, it seems more fruitful to treat them as distinct but complementary lines of action. For example, simply designating certain social and economic development endeavors indirect teaching may cause confusion in at least two ways: On the one hand, it may give the impression that development activities should have as their primary and immediate objective the recruitment of new believers, which is, of course, not the case. On the other, it may suggest to some friends that they are fulfilling their obligation to teach merely by participating in social action.

Social and economic development is an important area of activity in and of itself. Its justification should not be sought in its ability to produce enrollments; it complements teaching and also contributes to it. Naturally, when endeavors in the development field are successful, they increase the public's interest in the Faith and create new teaching opportunities for the Bahá'í community, opportunities which the friends should seize upon through their expansion and consolidation activities.

(The Universal House of Justice, from a memorandum dated 27 April 1998 to the Office of Social and Economic Development) [116]

One of the basic principles governing Bahá'í social and economic development is that the friends should give the Teachings of Bahá'u'lláh liberally and unconditionally to humanity so that people everywhere can apply them to pressing social issues and improve their individual and collective lives, both in material and spiritual dimensions. Access to the Word of God should not be conditioned upon acceptance of Bahá'u'lláh as a Manifestation of God for today. Moreover, it would not be inappropriate to refrain from explicitly mentioning the Source of inspiration underlying an educational programme developed on the basis of His Teachings, when circumstances demand it. In this light, there are a range of options that the friends can consider when creating educational materials which draw on the teachings and principles of the Faith.

(From a letter dated 11 June 2006 written on behalf of the Universal House of Justice to an individual believer) [117]

It is to be expected that a desire to undertake social action will accompany the collective change which begins to occur in a village or neighbourhood as acts of communal worship and home visits are woven together with activities for the spiritual education of its population to create a rich pattern of community life. Social action can, of course, range from the most informal efforts of limited duration to social and economic development programmes of a high level of complexity and sophistication promoted by Bahá'í-inspired non-governmental organizations—all concerned with the application of the teachings to some need identified in such fields as health, education, agriculture and the environment.

(From a letter dated 4 January 2009 written on behalf of the Universal House of Justice to a National Spiritual Assembly) [118]

In our Riḍván 2008 message we indicated that, as the friends continued to labour at the level of the cluster, they would find themselves drawn further and further into the life of society and would be challenged to extend the process of systematic learning in which they are engaged to encompass a widening range of human endeavours. A rich tapestry of community life begins to emerge in every cluster as acts of communal worship, interspersed with discussions undertaken in the intimate setting of the home, are woven together with activities that provide spiritual education to all members of the population—adults, youth and children. Social consciousness is heightened naturally as, for example, lively conversations proliferate among parents regarding the aspirations of their children and service projects spring up at the initiative of junior youth. Once human resources in a cluster are in sufficient abundance, and the pattern of growth firmly established, the community's engagement with society can, and indeed must, increase. At this crucial point in the unfoldment of the Plan, when so many clusters are nearing such a stage, it seems appropriate that the friends everywhere would reflect on the nature of the contributions which their growing, vibrant communities will make to the material and spiritual progress of society. In this respect, it will prove fruitful to think in terms of two interconnected, mutually reinforcing areas of activity: involvement in social action and participation in the prevalent discourses of society. . . .

Most appropriately conceived in terms of a spectrum, social action can range from fairly informal efforts of limited duration undertaken by individuals or small groups of friends to programmes of social and economic development with a high level of complexity and sophistication implemented by Bahá'í-inspired organizations. Irrespective of its scope and scale, all social action seeks to apply the teachings and principles of the Faith to improve some aspect of the social or economic life of a population, however modestly. Such endeavours are distinguished, then, by their stated purpose to promote the material well-being of the population, in addition to its spiritual welfare. That the world civilization now on humanity's horizon must achieve a dynamic coherence between the material and spiritual requirements of life is central to the Bahá'í teachings. Clearly this ideal has profound implications for the nature of any social action pursued by Bahá'ís, whatever its scope and range of influence. Though conditions will vary from country to country, and perhaps from cluster to cluster, eliciting from the friends a variety of endeavours, there are certain fundamental concepts that all should bear in mind. One is the centrality of knowledge to social existence. The perpetuation of ignorance is a most grievous form of oppression; it reinforces the many walls of prejudice that stand as barriers to the realization of the oneness of humankind, at once the goal and operating principle of Bahá'u'lláh's Revelation. Access to knowledge is the right of every human being, and participation in its generation, application and diffusion a responsibility that all must shoulder in the great enterprise of building a prosperous world civilization— each individual according to his or her talents and abilities. Justice demands universal participation. Thus, while social action may involve the provision of goods and services in some form, its primary concern must be to build capacity within a given population to participate in creating a better world. Social change is not a project that one group of people carries out for the benefit of another. The scope and complexity of social action must be commensurate with the human resources available in a village or neighbourhood to carry it forward. Efforts best begin, then, on a modest scale and grow organically as capacity within the population develops. Capacity rises to new levels, of course, as the protagonists of social change learn to apply with increasing effectiveness elements of Bahá'u'lláh's Revelation, together with the contents and methods of science, to their social reality. This reality they must strive to read in a manner consistent with His teachings—seeing in their fellow human beings gems of inestimable value and recognizing the effects of the dual process of integration and disintegration on both hearts and minds, as well as on social structures. . . .

. . . Further involvement in the life of society should not be sought prematurely. It will proceed naturally as the friends in every cluster persevere in applying the provisions of the Plan through a process of action, reflection, consultation and study, and learn as a result. Involvement in the life of society will flourish as the capacity of the community to promote its own growth and to maintain its vitality is gradually raised. It will achieve coherence with efforts to expand and consolidate the community to the extent that it draws on elements of the conceptual framework which governs the current series of global Plans. And it will contribute to the movement of populations towards Bahá'u'lláh's vision of a prosperous and peaceful world civilization to the degree that it employs these elements creatively in new areas of learning.

(The Universal House of Justice, Riḍván 2010 message to the Bahá'ís of the World)   [119]

While expansion and consolidation have steadily progressed over the past year, other important areas of activity have also moved forward, often in close parallel. As a prime example, the advances at the level of culture being witnessed in some villages and neighbourhoods are due in no small part to what is being learned from Bahá'í involvement in social action. Our Office of Social and Economic Development recently prepared a document which distils thirty years of experience that has accumulated in this field since that Office was established at the Bahá'í World Centre. Among the observations it makes is that efforts to engage in social action are lent vital impetus by the training institute. This is not simply through the rise in human resources it fosters. The spiritual insights, qualities, and abilities that are cultivated by the institute process have proven to be as crucial for participation in social action as they are for contributing to the process of growth. Further, it is explained how the Bahá'í community's distinct spheres of endeavour are governed by a common, evolving, conceptual framework composed of mutually reinforcing elements, albeit these assume varied expressions in different domains of action. The document we have described was lately shared with National Spiritual Assemblies, and we invite them, in consultation with the Counsellors, to consider how the concepts it explores can help to enhance existing efforts of social action pursued under their auspices and raise consciousness of this significant dimension of Bahá'í endeavour.[3] This should not be interpreted as a general call for widespread activity in this area—the

---

3. "Social Action: A paper prepared by the Office of Social and Economic Development at the Bahá'í World Centre, 26 November 2012," published in *Framework for Action: Selected Messages of the Universal House of Justice and Supplementary Material, 2006–2016* (West Palm Beach: Palabra Publications, 2017), pp. 327–50. It is also available on the Bahá'í Reference Library.

emergence of social action happens naturally, as a growing community gathers strength—but it is timely that the friends reflect more deeply on the implications of their exertions for the transformation of society. The surge in learning that is occurring in this field places increased demands upon the Office of Social and Economic Development, and steps are being taken to ensure that its functioning evolves commensurately.

(The Universal House of Justice, Riḍván 2013 message to the Bahá'ís of the World) [120]

In recent years it has become evident that in communities where there has been a strong emphasis on the capacity-building features of the Five Year Plan, the ability of the friends to engage in social action has increased substantially. Accordingly, you would do well to encourage the friends to persevere in their efforts to strengthen the training institute and the activities of the Plan, for therein lies the key to multiplying your human resources and creating a vibrant, united, and loving community. As they progress along this path, they will become increasingly capable of contributing in tangible ways to the practical resolution of the problems that confront populations at the grassroots in cities and towns, neighbourhoods and villages.

(From a letter dated 1 October 2015 written on behalf of the Universal House of Justice to a National Spiritual Assembly) [121]

A natural outcome of the rise both in resources and in consciousness of the implications of the Revelation for the life of a population is the stirrings of social action. Not infrequently, initiatives of this kind emerge organically out of the junior youth spiritual empowerment programme or are prompted by consultations about local conditions that occur at community gatherings. The forms that such endeavours can assume are diverse and include, for example, tutorial assistance to children, projects to better the physical environment, and activities to improve health and prevent disease. Some initiatives become sustained and gradually grow. In various places the founding of a community school at the grassroots has arisen from a heightened concern for the proper education of children and awareness of its importance, flowing naturally from the study of institute materials. On occasion, the efforts of the friends can be greatly reinforced through the work of an established Bahá'í-inspired organization functioning in the vicinity. However humble an instance of social action might be at the beginning, it is an indication of a people cultivating within themselves a critical capacity, one that holds infinite potential and significance for the centuries ahead: learning how to apply the Revelation to the manifold dimensions of social existence. All such initiatives also serve to enrich participation, at an individual and collective level, in prevalent discourses of the wider community. As expected, the friends are being drawn further into the life of society—a development which is inherent in the pattern of action in a cluster from the very start, but which is now much more pronounced.

> (The Universal House of Justice, from a message dated 29 December 2015 to the Conference of the Continental Boards of Counsellors)   [122]

Generally speaking, Bahá'í development projects begin at the grassroots and are, in the early stages, sustained by locally available human and financial resources. If such projects are introduced prematurely in a cluster, they risk distracting and dissipating the energies of the friends who should be attending primarily to advancing the process of expansion and consolidation. In this regard, experience has shown that community schools, like other efforts of social action, have proven more sustainable when they emerge in localities with a strong institute process, as a natural extension of the community-building activities under way. In these localities, conditions for starting a school are fostered as growing numbers of people participate in the study of the main sequence of institute courses, which serves to equip more and more individuals with the qualities, attitudes, and skills required to contribute to processes of spiritual and material transformation. Further, when efforts to multiply and strengthen children's classes and junior youth groups foster a community's sense of ownership for the education of younger generations, they lead to an increase in collective capacity to implement even more complex endeavours.

(From a letter dated 9 April 2017 written on behalf of the Universal House of Justice to a National Spiritual Assembly) [123]

As the work of community building intensifies, the friends are using the new capacities they have developed to improve conditions in the society around them, their enthusiasm kindled by their study of the divine teachings. Short-term projects have soared in number, formal programmes have expanded their reach, and there are now more Bahá'í-inspired development organizations engaged in education, health, agriculture, and other areas. From the resulting transformation visible in the individual and collective lives of peoples may be discerned the unmistakable stirrings of the society-building power of the Cause of Bahá'u'lláh. No wonder, then, that it is from such instances of social action—whether simple or complex, of fixed duration or long sustained—that the Offices of the Bahá'í International Community are increasingly taking inspiration in their efforts to participate in the prevalent discourses of society.

(The Universal House of Justice, Riḍván 2018 message to the Bahá'ís of the World) [124]

During the ministries of 'Abdu'l-Bahá and Shoghi Effendi, the first community of sufficient size that could begin to systematically apply Bahá'u'lláh's teachings to unite material and spiritual progress was that of the believers in the Cradle of the Faith. The steady flow of guidance from the Holy Land enabled the Bahá'ís of Iran to make tremendous strides in but one or two generations and to contribute a distinctive share to the progress of their nation. A network of schools that provided moral and academic education, including for girls, flourished. Illiteracy was virtually eliminated in the Bahá'í community. Philanthropic enterprises were created. Prejudices among ethnic and religious groups, aflame in the wider society, were extinguished within the community's loving embrace. Villages became distinguished for their cleanliness, order, and progress. And believers from that land were instrumental in raising in another land the first Mashriqu'l-Adhkár with its dependencies designed to "afford relief to the suffering, sustenance to the poor, shelter to the wayfarer, solace to the bereaved, and education to the ignorant." Over time, such efforts were augmented by scattered initiatives of other Bahá'í communities in various parts of the world. However, as Shoghi Effendi remarked to one community, the number of believers was as yet too small to effect a notable change in the wider society, and for more than the first half century of the Formative Age the believers were encouraged to concentrate their energies on the propagation of the Faith, since this was work that only Bahá'ís could do—indeed their primary spiritual obligation—and it would prepare them for the time when they could address the problems of humanity more directly.

Thirty-five years ago, circumstances within and outside the community combined to create new possibilities for greater involvement in the life of society. The Faith had developed to the stage at which the processes of social and economic development needed to be incorporated into its regular pursuits, and in October 1983 we called upon the Bahá'ís of the world to enter this new field of endeavor. The Office of Social and Economic Development was established at the Bahá'í World Centre to assist us in promoting and coordinating the activities of the friends worldwide. Bahá'í activities for social and economic development, at whatever level of complexity, were at that time counted in the hundreds. Today they number in the tens of thousands, including hundreds of sustained projects such as schools and scores of development organizations. The broad range of current activities spans efforts from villages and neighborhoods to regions and nations, addressing an array of challenges, including education from preschool to university, literacy, health, the environment, support for refugees, advancement of women, empowerment of junior youth, elimination of racial prejudice, agriculture, local economies, and village development. The society-building power of Bahá'u'lláh's Cause has begun to be more systematically expressed in the collective life of the friends as a result of the acceleration of the process of expansion and consolidation, especially in advanced clusters. Beyond this, of course, countless believers, through their professional and voluntary efforts, contribute their energies and insights to projects and organizations established for the common good.

Once again, then, we find that forces inside and outside the Faith have made possible a new stage in the work of social and economic development in the Bahá'í world. Therefore, on this sacred occasion of the Festivals of the Twin Birthdays, we are pleased to announce that the Office of Social and Economic Development now effloresces into a new world-embracing institution established at the World Centre, the Bahá'í International Development Organization. In addition, a Bahá'í Development Fund will be inaugurated, from which the new organization will draw to assist both long-standing and emerging development efforts worldwide; it will be supported by the House of Justice, and individuals and institutions may contribute to it.

(The Universal House of Justice, from a message dated 9 November 2018 to the Bahá'ís of the World) [125]

Community Development and the Movement of Populations

O people of the world! Build ye houses of worship throughout the lands in the name of Him Who is the Lord of all religions. Make them as perfect as is possible in the world of being, and adorn them with that which befitteth them, not with images and effigies. Then, with radiance and joy, celebrate therein the praise of your Lord, the Most Compassionate. Verily, by His remembrance the eye is cheered and the heart is filled with light.

(Bahá'u'lláh, The Kitáb-i-Aqdas, ¶31) [126]

. . . all the members of the human family, whether peoples or governments, cities or villages, have become increasingly interdependent. For none is self-sufficiency any longer possible, inasmuch as political ties unite all peoples and nations, and the bonds of trade and industry, of agriculture and education, are being strengthened every day. Hence the unity of all mankind can in this day be achieved.

('Abdu'l-Bahá, Selections from the Writings of 'Abdu'l-Bahá, no. 15.6) [127]

Although to outward seeming the Mashriqu'l-Adhkár is a material structure, yet it hath a spiritual effect. It forgeth bonds of unity from heart to heart; it is a collective center for men's souls. Every city in which, during the days of the Manifestation, a temple was raised up, hath created security and constancy and peace, for such buildings were given over to the perpetual glorification of God, and only in the remembrance of God can the heart find rest. Gracious God! The edifice of the House of Worship hath a powerful influence on every phase of life. Experience hath, in the east, clearly shown this to be a fact. Even if, in some small village, a house was designated as the Mashriqu'l-Adhkár, it produced a marked effect; how much greater would be the impact of one especially raised up.

> ('Abdu'l-Bahá, *Selections from the Writings of 'Abdu'l-Bahá*, no. 60.1) [128]

The Mashriqu'l-Adhkár is one of the most vital institutions in the world, and it hath many subsidiary branches. Although it is a House of Worship, it is also connected with a hospital, a drug dispensary, a traveler's hospice, a school for orphans, and a university for advanced studies. Every Mashriqu'l-Adhkár is connected with these five things. My hope is that the Mashriqu'l-Adhkár will now be established in America, and that gradually the hospital, the school, the university, the dispensary and the hospice, all functioning according to the most efficient and orderly procedures, will follow. Make these matters known to the beloved of the Lord, so that they will understand how very great is the importance of this "Dawning-Point of the Remembrance of God." The Temple is not only a place for worship; rather, in every respect is it complete and whole.

> ('Abdu'l-Bahá, *Selections from the Writings of 'Abdu'l-Bahá*, no. 64.1) [129]

The foundation of life and existence is cooperation and mutual aid, whereas the cause of annihilation and deterioration is the cessation of aid and assistance. The higher the realm of existence, the stronger and more vital this weighty matter of cooperation and assistance doth become. In the realm of humanity, therefore, cooperation and mutual aid are in a greater degree of completeness and perfection than that which prevaileth in the other realms of existence—so much so, that the life of humanity dependeth entirely upon this principle. Among the friends of God, in particular, this strong foundation must be fortified in such wise that each soul may help the other in all matters, whether pertaining to spiritual realities and inner truths or to the material and physical aspects of life. Such is especially the case with regard to the founding of public institutions that benefit all people, and, in particular, the Ma<u>sh</u>riqu'l-A<u>dh</u>kár, which constituteth the greatest of divine foundations.

('Abdu'l-Bahá, from a Tablet—translated from the Persian) [130]

The responsibilities of the members of the Spiritual Assemblies that are engaged in teaching the Cause of God in Eastern lands have been clearly laid down in the holy Texts.

These bid them to work towards the improvement of morals and the spread of learning; to strive to eradicate ignorance and unenlightenment, eliminate prejudice, and reinforce the foundation of true faith in people's hearts and minds; to seek to develop self-reliance and avoidance of blind imitation; to aim to enhance the efficient management of their affairs, and observe purity and refinement in all circumstances; to show their commitment to truthfulness and honesty, and their ability to conduct themselves with frankness, courage and resolution.

They similarly enjoin them to lend their support to agricultural and industrial development, to consolidate the foundations of mutual assistance and co-operation, to promote the emancipation and advancement of women and support the compulsory education of both sexes, to encourage application of the principles of consultation among all classes, and to adhere in all dealings to a standard of scrupulous integrity.

(Shoghi Effendi, from a letter dated 30 January 1926 written to the Local Spiritual Assemblies of the East—translated from the Persian)   [131]

There are, at the present time, many villages in India, the Philippines, Africa, Latin America, etc., where the Bahá'ís form a majority or even the entire population of the village. One of the goals of the Five Year Plan, as you will recall, is to develop the characteristics of Bahá'í community life, and it is, above all, to such villages that the goal is directed. The Local Spiritual Assemblies of such villages must gradually widen the scope of their activities, not only to develop every aspect of the spiritual life of the believers within their jurisdiction, but also, through Bahá'í consultation, and through such Bahá'í principles as harmony between science and religion, the importance of education, and work as a form of worship, to promote the standards of agriculture and other skills in the life of the people. For this they will need the assistance of Bahá'í experts from other lands. This is a major undertaking, and is being started gradually wherever and whenever possible.

(From a letter dated 27 July 1976 written on behalf of the Universal House of Justice to an individual believer)   [132]

When the Bahá'í community in a village is a significant proportion of the population, it has a wide range of opportunities to be an example and an encouragement of means of improving the quality of life in the village. Among the initiatives which it might take are measures to foster child education, adult literacy and the training of women to better discharge their responsibilities as mothers and to play an enlarged role in the administrative and social life of the village; encouragement of the people of the village to join together in devotions, perhaps in the early morning, irrespective of their varieties of religious belief; support of efforts to improve the hygiene and the health of the village, including attention to the provision of pure water, the preservation of cleanliness in the village environment, and education in the harmful effects of narcotic and intoxicating substances. No doubt other possibilities will present themselves to the village Bahá'í community and its Local Spiritual Assembly.

(From a letter dated 25 July 1988 written on behalf of the Universal House of Justice to a National Spiritual Assembly) [133]

A community is of course more than the sum of its membership; it is a comprehensive unit of civilization composed of individuals, families and institutions that are originators and encouragers of systems, agencies and organizations working together with a common purpose for the welfare of people both within and beyond its own borders; it is a composition of diverse, interacting participants that are achieving unity in an unremitting quest for spiritual and social progress. Since Bahá'ís everywhere are at the very beginning of the process of community building, enormous effort must be devoted to the tasks at hand.

As we have said in an earlier message, the flourishing of the community, especially at the local level, demands a significant enhancement in patterns of behaviour: those patterns by which the collective expression of the virtues of the individual members and the functioning of the Spiritual Assembly are manifest in the unity and fellowship of the community and the dynamism of its activity and growth. This calls for the integration of the component elements—adults, youth and children—in spiritual, social, educational and administrative activities; and their engagement in local plans of teaching and development. It implies a collective will and sense of purpose to perpetuate the Spiritual Assembly through annual elections. It involves the practice of collective worship of God. Hence, it is essential to the spiritual life of the community that the friends hold regular devotional meetings in local Bahá'í centres, where available, or elsewhere, including the homes of believers.

(The Universal House of Justice, Riḍván 1996 message to the Bahá'ís of the World) [134]

As you are aware, often in a rural cluster made up of villages and perhaps one or two towns, while the pattern of action associated with an intensive programme of growth is being established, the efforts of the friends are confined to a few localities. Once in place, however, the pattern can be extended quickly to village after village, as explained in our Riḍván message this year. Early on in each locality, the Local Spiritual Assembly comes into existence, and its steady development follows a trajectory parallel with, and intimately tied to, the fledgling process of growth unfolding in the village. And not unlike the evolution of other facets of this process, the development of the Local Assembly can best be understood in terms of capacity building.

What needs to occur in the first instance is relatively straightforward: Individual awareness of the process of growth gathering momentum in the village, born of each member's personal involvement in the core activities, must coalesce into a collective consciousness that recognizes both the nature of the transformation under way and the obligation of the Assembly to foster it. Without doubt, some attention will have to be given to certain basic administrative functions—for example, meeting with a degree of regularity, conducting the Nineteen Day Feast and planning Holy Day observances, establishing a local fund, and holding annual elections in accordance with Bahá'í principle. However, it should not prove difficult for the Local Assembly to begin, concomitant with such efforts and with encouragement from an assistant to an Auxiliary Board member, to consult as a body on one or two specific issues with immediate relevance to the life of the community: how the devotional character of the village is being enhanced through the efforts of individuals who have completed the first institute course; how the spiritual education of the children is being addressed by teachers raised up by the institute; how the potential of junior youth is being realized by the programme for their spiritual empowerment; how the spiritual and social fabric of the community is being strengthened as the friends visit one another in their homes. As the Assembly consults on such tangible matters and learns to nurture the process of growth lovingly and patiently, its relationship with the Area Teaching Committee and the training institute gradually becomes cemented in a common purpose. But, of still greater importance, it will begin to lay the foundations on which can be built that uniquely affectionate and genuinely supportive relationship, described by the beloved Guardian in many of his messages, which Local Spiritual Assemblies should establish with the individual believer.

Clearly, learning to consult on specific issues related to the global Plan, no matter how crucial, represents but one dimension of the capacity-building process in which the Local Spiritual Assembly must engage. Its continued development implies adherence to the injunction laid down by 'Abdu'l-Bahá that "discussions must all be confined to spiritual matters that pertain to the training of souls, the instruction of children, the relief of the poor, the help of the feeble throughout all classes in the world, kindness to all peoples, the diffusion of the fragrances of God and the exaltation of His Holy Word." Its steady advancement requires an unbending commitment to promote the best interests of the community and a vigilance in guarding the process of growth against the forces of moral decay that threaten to arrest it. Its ongoing progress calls for a sense of responsibility that extends beyond the circle of friends and families engaged in the core activities to encompass the entire population of the village. And sustaining its gradual maturation is unshakable faith in 'Abdu'l-Bahá's assurance that He will enfold every Spiritual Assembly within the embrace of His care and protection.

Associated with this rise in collective consciousness is the Assembly's growing ability to properly assess and utilize resources, financial and otherwise, both in support of community activities and in discharging its administrative functions, which may in time include the judicious appointment of committees and the maintenance of modest physical facilities for its operations. No less vital is its ability to nurture an environment conducive to the participation of large numbers in unified action and to ensure that their energies and talents contribute towards progress. In all these respects, the spiritual well-being of the community remains uppermost in the Assembly's mind. And when inevitable problems arise, whether in relation to some activity or among individuals, they will be addressed by a Local Spiritual Assembly which has so completely gained the confidence of the members of the community that all naturally turn to it for assistance. This implies that the Assembly has learned through experience how to help the believers put aside the divisive ways of a partisan mindset, how to find the seeds of unity in even the most perplexing and thorny situations and how to nurture them slowly and lovingly, upholding at all times the standard of justice.

As the community grows in size and in capacity to maintain vitality, the friends will, we have indicated in the past, be drawn further into the life of society and be challenged to take advantage of the approaches they have developed to respond to a widening range of issues that face their village. The question of coherence, so essential to the growth achieved thus far, and so fundamental to the Plan's evolving framework for action, now assumes new dimensions. Much will fall on the Local Assembly, not as an executor of projects but as the voice of moral authority, to make certain that, as the friends strive to apply the teachings of the Faith to improve conditions through a process of action, reflection and consultation, the integrity of their endeavours is not compromised.

Our Riḍván message described a few of the characteristics of social action at the grassroots, and the conditions it must meet. Efforts in a village will generally begin on a small scale, perhaps with the emergence of groups of friends, each concerned with a specific social or economic need it has identified and each pursuing a simple set of appropriate actions. Consultation at the Nineteen Day Feast creates a space for the growing social consciousness of the community to find constructive expression. Whatever the nature of activities undertaken, the Local Assembly must be attentive to potential pitfalls and help the friends, if necessary, to steer past them—the allurements of overly ambitious projects that would consume energies and ultimately prove untenable, the temptation of financial grants that would necessitate a departure from Bahá'í principle, the promises of technologies deceptively packaged that would strip the village of its cultural heritage and lead to fragmentation and dissonance. Eventually the strength of the institute process in the village, and the enhanced capabilities it has fostered in individuals, may enable the friends to take advantage of methods and programmes of proven effectiveness, which have been developed by one or another Bahá'í-inspired organization and which have been introduced into the cluster at the suggestion of, and with support from, our Office of Social and Economic Development. Moreover, the Assembly must learn to interact with social and political structures in the locality, gradually raising consciousness of the presence of the Faith and the influence it is exerting on the progress of the village.

What is outlined in the foregoing paragraphs represents only a few of the attributes which Local Spiritual Assemblies in the many villages of the world will gradually develop in serving the needs of communities that embrace larger and larger numbers. As they increasingly manifest their latent capacities and powers, their members will come to be seen by the inhabitants of each village as "the trusted ones of the Merciful among men." Thus will these Assemblies become "shining lamps and heavenly gardens, from which the fragrances of holiness are diffused over all regions, and the lights of knowledge are shed abroad over all created things. From them the spirit of life streameth in every direction."

> (The Universal House of Justice, from a message dated 28 December 2010 to the Conference of the Continental Boards of Counsellors) [135]

From this landscape of thriving activity, one prospect deserves particular mention. In the message addressed to you three years ago, we expressed the hope that, in clusters with an intensive programme of growth in operation, the friends would endeavour to learn more about the ways of community building by developing centres of intense activity in neighbourhoods and villages. Our hopes have been exceeded, for even in clusters where the programme of growth has not yet achieved intensity, efforts by a few to initiate core activities among the residents of small areas have demonstrated their efficacy time and again. In essence, this approach centres on the response to Bahá'u'lláh's teachings on the part of populations who are ready for the spiritual transformation His Revelation fosters. Through participation in the educational process promoted by the training institute, they are motivated to reject the torpor and indifference inculcated by the forces of society and pursue, instead, patterns of action which prove life altering. Where this approach has advanced for some years in a neighbourhood or village and the friends have sustained their focus, remarkable results are becoming gradually but unmistakably evident. Youth are empowered to take responsibility for the development of those around them younger than themselves. Older generations welcome the contribution of the youth to meaningful discussions about the affairs of the whole community. For young and old alike, the discipline cultivated through the community's educational process builds capacity for consultation, and new spaces emerge for purposeful conversation. Yet change is not confined merely to the Bahá'ís and those who are involved in the core activities called for by the Plan, who might reasonably be expected to adopt new ways of thinking over time. The very spirit of the place is affected. A devotional attitude takes shape within a broad sweep of the population. Expressions of the equality of men and women become more pronounced. The education of children, both boys and girls, commands greater attention. The character of relationships within families—moulded by assumptions centuries old—alters perceptibly. A sense of duty towards one's immediate community and physical environment becomes prevalent. Even the scourge of prejudice, which casts its baleful shadow on every society, begins to yield to the compelling force of unity. In short, the community-building work in which the friends are engaged influences aspects of culture.

(The Universal House of Justice, Riḍván 2013 message to the Bahá'ís of the World) [136]

A House of Worship is, of course, an integral part of the process of community building, and its construction represents an important milestone in the development of a community. It is the hope of the House of Justice that the friends in . . . will, through the zeal and determination with which they pursue the essential activities of the Five Year Plan, hasten the day when it will be timely for a Mashriqu'l-Adhkár to be built in your country.

(From a letter dated 12 December 2013 written on behalf of the Universal House of Justice to an individual believer) [137]

Underlying the process even from the start is, of course, a collective movement towards the vision of material and spiritual prosperity set forth by Him Who is the Lifegiver of the World. But when such large numbers are involved, the movement of an entire population becomes discernible.

This movement is especially in evidence in those clusters where a local Mashriqu'l-Adhkár is to be established. One such, by way of example, is in Vanuatu. The friends who reside on the island of Tanna have made a supreme effort to raise consciousness of the planned House of Worship, and have already engaged no less than a third of the island's 30,000 inhabitants in an expanding conversation about its significance in a variety of ways. The ability to sustain an elevated conversation among so many people has been refined through years of experience sharing the teachings of Bahá'u'lláh and extending the reach of a vibrant training institute. Junior youth groups on the island are particularly thriving, urged on by the support of village chiefs who see how the participants are spiritually empowered. Encouraged by the unity and dedication that exist among them, these young people have not only dispelled the languor of passivity in themselves but have, through various practical projects, found means to work for the betterment of their community, and as a result, those of all ages, not least their own parents, have been galvanized into constructive action. Among the believers and the wider society, the bounty of being able to turn to a Local Spiritual Assembly for guidance and for the resolution of difficult situations is being recognized, and in turn, the decisions of the Spiritual Assemblies are increasingly characterized by wisdom and sensitivity. There is much here to indicate that, when the elements of the Plan's framework for action are combined into a coherent whole, the impact on a population can be profound. And it is against the background of ongoing expansion and consolidation—the thirtieth

cycle of the intensive programme of growth has recently concluded—
that the friends are actively exploring, with the rest of the island's
inhabitants, what it means for a Mashriqu'l-Adhkár, a "collective centre for men's souls," to be raised up in their midst. With the active
support of traditional leaders, Tanna islanders have offered no less than
a hundred design ideas for the Temple, demonstrating the extent to
which the House of Worship has captured imaginations, and opening
up enthralling prospects for the influence it is set to exert on the lives
lived beneath its shade.

> (The Universal House of Justice, Riḍván 2014 message to the
> Baháʼís of the World)   [138]

. . . a House of Worship is to be the spiritual centre of a community
and, together with its dependencies that will be created, contributes
to a flourishing pattern of collective life. Currently, the first Houses
of Worship of each continent serve as the national Temples of the
countries in which they are located, and they also serve the communities in their vicinity, playing a significant role in local activities. As
the process of growth unfolds, Temples will increasingly be raised at
the national and local levels, and much will be learned about their
nature and how they contribute to the community-building process.
The many aspects of the functioning of this institution will then gradually be manifest. As Shoghi Effendi wrote, "None save the institution
of the Mashriqu'l-Adhkár can most adequately provide the essentials
of Baháʼí worship and service, both so vital to the regeneration of the
world."

> (From a letter dated 26 January 2015 written on behalf of the
> Universal House of Justice to an individual believer)   [139]

In some of the clusters where growth has advanced to this extent,
an even more thrilling development has occurred. There are loca-

tions within these clusters where a significant percentage of the entire population is now involved in community-building activities. For instance, there are small villages where the institute has been able to engage the participation of all the children and junior youth in its programmes. When the reach of activity is extensive, the societal impact of the Faith becomes more evident. The Bahá'í community is afforded higher standing as a distinctive moral voice in the life of a people and is able to contribute an informed perspective to the discourses around it on, say, the development of the younger generations. Figures of authority from the wider society start to draw on the insight and experience arising from initiatives of social action inspired by Bahá'u'lláh's teachings. Conversations influenced by those teachings, concerned with the common weal, permeate an ever-broader cross section of the population, to the point where an effect on the general discourse in a locality can be perceived. Beyond the Bahá'í community, people are coming to regard the Local Spiritual Assembly as a radiant source of wisdom to which they too can turn for illumination.

We recognize that developments like these are yet a distant prospect for many, even in clusters where the pattern of activity embraces large numbers. But in some places, this is the work of the moment. In such clusters, while the friends continue to be occupied with sustaining the process of growth, other dimensions of Bahá'í endeavour claim an increasing share of their attention. They are seeking to understand how a flourishing local population can transform the society of which it is an integral part. This will be a new frontier of learning for the foreseeable future, where insights will be generated that will ultimately benefit the whole Bahá'í world.

(The Universal House of Justice, from a message dated 29 December 2015 to the Conference of the Continental Boards of Counsellors) [140]

. . . as the work in thousands of villages and neighbourhoods gathers momentum, a vibrant community life is taking root in each. The number of clusters where the system for extending this pattern of activity to more and more locations is becoming well established—enabling, thereby, the friends to pass the third milestone along a continuum of development—has grown markedly. And it is here, at the frontiers of the Bahá'í world's learning, particularly in the movement of populations towards the vision of Bahá'u'lláh, where not only are large numbers coming into the widening embrace of Bahá'í activities but the friends are now learning how sizeable groups come to identify themselves with the community of the Most Great Name. We are seeing the Faith's educational efforts take on a more formal character in such places, as children move seamlessly through the grades year after year and one level of the junior youth spiritual empowerment programme reliably succeeds another. In these places, the training institute is learning to ensure that sufficient human resources are being raised up to provide for the spiritual and moral edification of children and junior youth in ever-increasing numbers. Participation in these foundational activities is becoming so embedded in the culture of the population that it is viewed as an indispensable aspect of the life of a community. A new vitality emerges within a people taking charge of their own development, and they build immunity to those societal forces that breed passivity. Possibilities for material and spiritual progress take shape. Social reality begins to transform.

(The Universal House of Justice, Riḍván 2018 message to the Bahá'ís of the World) [141]

METHODS AND APPROACHES

Learning and Systematic Action

The purpose of learning should be the promotion of the welfare of the people. . . . True learning is that which is conducive to the well-being of the world, not to pride and self-conceit, or to tyranny, violence and pillage.

(Bahá'u'lláh, from a Tablet—translated from the Persian) [142]

. . . the happiness and greatness, the rank and station, the pleasure and peace, of an individual have never consisted in his personal wealth, but rather in his excellent character, his high resolve, the breadth of his learning, and his ability to solve difficult problems.

('Abdu'l-Bahá, *The Secret of Divine Civilization*, ¶44)   [143]

There are certain pillars which have been established as the unshakable supports of the Faith of God. The mightiest of these is learning and the use of the mind, the expansion of consciousness, and insight into the realities of the universe and the hidden mysteries of Almighty God.

To promote knowledge is thus an inescapable duty imposed on every one of the friends of God.

('Abdu'l-Bahá, *Selections from the Writings of 'Abdu'l-Bahá*, no. 97.1–2)   [144]

All blessings are divine in origin, but none can be compared with this power of intellectual investigation and research, which is an eternal gift producing fruits of unending delight. . . . Therefore, you should put forward your most earnest efforts toward the acquisition of science and arts. The greater your attainment, the higher your standard in the divine purpose. The man of science is perceiving and endowed with vision, whereas he who is ignorant and neglectful of this development is blind. The investigating mind is attentive, alive; the callous and indifferent mind is deaf and dead. A scientific man is a true index and representative of humanity, for through processes of inductive reasoning and research he is informed of all that appertains to humanity, its status, conditions and happenings. He studies the human body politic, understands social problems and weaves the web and texture of civilization. In fact, science may be likened to a mirror wherein the infinite forms and images of existing things are revealed and reflected. It is the very foundation of all individual and national development. Without this basis of investigation, development is impossible. Therefore, seek with diligent endeavor the knowledge and attainment of all that lies within the power of this wonderful bestowal.

('Abdu'l-Bahá, *The Promulgation of Universal Peace*, pp. 67–68)
[145]

The present condition of the world—its economic instability, social dissensions, political dissatisfaction and international distrust—should awaken the youth from their slumber and make them enquire what the future is going to bring. It is surely they who will suffer most if some calamity sweep over the world. They should therefore open their eyes to the existing conditions, study the evil forces that are at play and then with a concerted effort arise and bring about the necessary reforms—

reforms that shall contain within their scope the spiritual as well as social and political phases of human life.

> (From a letter dated 13 March 1932 written on behalf of Shoghi Effendi to an individual believer) [146]

Systematization ensures consistency of lines of action based on well-conceived plans. In a general sense, it implies an orderliness of approach in all that pertains to Bahá'í service, whether in teaching or administration, in individual or collective endeavour. While allowing for individual initiative and spontaneity, it suggests the need to be clear-headed, methodical, efficient, constant, balanced and harmonious. Systematization is a necessary mode of functioning animated by the urgency to act.

> (The Universal House of Justice, Riḍván 1998 message to the Bahá'ís of the World) [147]

If learning is to be the primary mode of operation in a community, then visions, strategies, goals and methods have to be re-examined time and again. As tasks are accomplished, obstacles removed, resources multiplied and lessons learned, modifications have to be made in goals and approaches, but in a way that continuity of action is maintained.

> (*The Institution of the Counsellors*, a document prepared by the Universal House of Justice (Haifa: Bahá'í World Centre, 2001), p. 24) [148]

One of your primary concerns will be to strengthen appreciation for systematic action, already heightened by the successes it has brought. To arrive at a unified vision of growth based on a realistic assessment of possibilities and resources, to develop strategies that lend structure to it, to devise and implement plans of action commensurate with capacity, to make necessary adjustments while maintaining continuity, to build on accomplishments—these are some of the requisites of systematization that every community must learn and internalize.

(The Universal House of Justice, from a message dated 27 December 2005 to the Conference of the Continental Boards of Counsellors) [149]

This evolution in collective consciousness is discernable in the growing frequency with which the word "accompany" appears in conversations among the friends, a word that is being endowed with new meaning as it is integrated into the common vocabulary of the Bahá'í community. It signals the significant strengthening of a culture in which learning is the mode of operation, a mode that fosters the informed participation of more and more people in a united effort to apply Bahá'u'lláh's teachings to the construction of a divine civilization, which the Guardian states is the primary mission of the Faith. Such an approach offers a striking contrast to the spiritually bankrupt and moribund ways of an old social order that so often seeks to harness human energy through domination, through greed, through guilt or through manipulation.

In relationships among the friends, then, this development in culture finds expression in the quality of their interactions. Learning as a mode of operation requires that all assume a posture of humility, a condition in which one becomes forgetful of self, placing complete trust in God, reliant on His all-sustaining power and confident in His unfailing assistance, knowing that He, and He alone, can change the gnat into an eagle, the drop into a boundless sea. And in such a state souls labour together ceaselessly, delighting not so much in their own accomplishments but in the progress and services of others. So it is that their thoughts are centred at all times on helping one another scale the heights of service to His Cause and soar in the heaven of His knowledge. This is what we see in the present pattern of activity unfolding across the globe, propagated by young and old, by veteran and newly enrolled, working side by side.

Not only does this advance in culture influence relations among individuals, but its effects can also be felt in the conduct of the administrative affairs of the Faith. As learning has come to distinguish the community's mode of operation, certain aspects of decision making related to expansion and consolidation have been assigned to the body of the believers, enabling planning and implementation to become more responsive to circumstances on the ground. . . .

Bahá'u'lláh's Revelation is vast. It calls for profound change not only at the level of the individual but also in the structure of society. "Is not the object of every Revelation," He Himself proclaims, "to effect a transformation in the whole character of mankind, a transformation that shall manifest itself, both outwardly and inwardly, that shall affect both its inner life and external conditions?" The work advancing in every corner of the globe today represents the latest stage of the ongoing Bahá'í endeavour to create the nucleus of the glorious civilization enshrined in His teachings, the building of which is an enterprise of infinite complexity and scale, one that will demand centuries of exertion by humanity to bring to fruition. There are no shortcuts, no formulas. Only as effort is made to draw on insights from His Revelation, to tap into the accumulating knowledge of the human race, to apply His teachings intelligently to the life of humanity, and to consult on the questions that arise will the necessary learning occur and capacity be developed.

(The Universal House of Justice, Riḍván 2010 message to the Bahá'ís of the World) [150]

Numerous, of course, are the questions that the process of learning, now under way in all regions of the world, must address: how to bring people of different backgrounds together in an environment which, devoid of the constant threat of conflict and distinguished by its devotional character, encourages them to put aside the divisive ways of a partisan mindset, fosters higher degrees of unity of thought and action, and elicits wholehearted participation; how to administer the affairs of a community in which there is no ruling class with priestly functions that can lay claim to distinction or privilege; how to enable contingents of men and women to break free from the confines of passivity and the chains of oppression in order to engage in activities conducive to their spiritual, social and intellectual development; how to help youth navigate through a crucial stage of their lives and become empowered to direct their energies towards the advancement of civilization; how to create dynamics within the family unit that lead to material and spiritual prosperity without instilling in the rising generations feelings of estrangement towards an illusory "other" or nurturing any instinct to exploit those relegated to this category; how to make it possible for decision making to benefit from a diversity of perspectives through a consultative process which, understood as the collective investigation of reality, promotes detachment from personal views, gives due importance to valid empirical information, does not raise mere opinion to the status of fact or define truth as the compromise between opposing interest groups. To explore questions such as these and the many others certain to arise, the Bahá'í community has adopted a mode of operation characterized by action, reflection, consultation and study—study which involves not only constant reference to the writings of the Faith but also the scientific analysis of patterns unfolding. Indeed, how to maintain such a mode of learning in action, how to ensure that growing numbers participate in the generation and application of relevant knowledge, and how to devise structures for the systemization of an expanding worldwide experience and for the equitable distribution of the lessons learned—these are, themselves, the object of regular examination.

The overall direction of the process of learning that the Bahá'í community is pursuing is guided by a series of global plans, the provisions of which are established by the Universal House of Justice. Capacity building is the watchword of these plans: they aim at enabling the protagonists of collective effort to strengthen the spiritual foundations of villages and neighbourhoods, to address certain of their social and economic needs, and to contribute to the discourses prevalent in society, all while maintaining the necessary coherence in methods and approaches.

(The Universal House of Justice, from a message dated 2 March 2013 to the Bahá'ís of Iran) [151]

Central to the effort to advance the work of expansion and consolidation, social action, and the involvement in the discourses of society is the notion of an evolving conceptual framework, a matrix that organizes thought and gives shape to activities and which becomes more elaborate as experience accumulates. It would be fruitful if the elements of this framework . . . can be consciously and progressively clarified. . . . Perhaps the most important of these is learning in action; the friends participate in an ongoing process of action, reflection, study, and consultation in order to address obstacles and share successes, re-examine and revise strategies and methods, and systematize and improve efforts over time.

(From a letter dated 24 July 2013 written on behalf of the Universal House of Justice to a National Spiritual Assembly) [152]

The Bahá'í approach to the questions you have raised is one which will be worked out over time through patient and persistent effort and by the process of learning in which the Bahá'í community is engaged. This process will be augmented by research and discussion and by attempts to correlate the teachings with modern thought, including the identification of similarities and distinctions between the teachings and contemporary social constructs. Involvement in the discourses of society by believers in various social spaces will sharpen the insights gained. Ongoing study of the teachings and systematic endeavour to translate Bahá'í principles into action by engaging in the processes of community building, education of children and youth, and social action will assist in refining our grasp of Bahá'u'lláh's intention for humanity in all areas of life. In the years ahead, the ability of the Bahá'í community to contribute to thought-shaping social change will increase, and answers to questions that appear to be unsolvable today will become apparent through a process of organic change, rather than as a result of imposing particular perspectives.

(From a letter dated 21 January 2014 written on behalf of the Universal House of Justice to an individual believer)   [153]

In many ways, the communities that have progressed furthest are tracing an inviting path for others to follow. Yet whatever the level of activity in a cluster, it is the capacity for learning among the local friends, within a common framework, that fosters progress along the path of development. Everyone has a share in this enterprise; the contribution of each serves to enrich the whole. The most dynamic clusters are those in which, irrespective of the resources the community possesses or the number of activities being undertaken, the friends appreciate that their task is to identify what is required for progress to occur—the nascent capacity that must be nurtured, the new skill that must be acquired, the initiators of a fledgling effort who must be accompanied, the space for reflection that must be cultivated, the collective endeavour that must be coordinated—and then find creative

ways in which the necessary time and resources can be made available
to achieve it. The very fact that each set of circumstances presents
its own challenges is enabling every community not simply to benefit
from what is being learned in the rest of the Bahá'í world but also to
add to that body of knowledge. Awareness of this reality frees one from
the fruitless search for a rigid formula for action while still allowing the
insights gleaned in diverse settings to inform the process of growth
as it takes a particular shape in one's own surroundings. This entire
approach is completely at odds with narrow conceptions of "success"
and "failure" that breed freneticism or paralyse volition. Detachment
is needed. When effort is expended wholly for the sake of God then all
that occurs belongs to Him and every victory won in His Name is an
occasion to celebrate His praise.

(The Universal House of Justice, Riḍván 2014 message to the
Bahá'ís of the World) [154]

. . . the capacity for learning, which represented such a priceless legacy
of previous Plans, is being extended beyond the realm of expansion and
consolidation to encompass other areas of Bahá'í endeavour, notably
social action and participation in the prevalent discourses of society.

(The Universal House of Justice, from a message dated
29 December 2015 to the Conference of the Continental
Boards of Counsellors) [155]

Consultation and Collaboration

O people of God! Give ear unto that which, if heeded, will ensure
the freedom, well-being, tranquility, exaltation and advancement of
all men. Certain laws and principles are necessary and indispensable
for Persia. However, it is fitting that these measures should be adopted
in conformity with the considered views of His Majesty—may God

aid him through His grace—and of the learned divines and of the high-ranking rulers. Subject to their approval a place should be fixed where they would meet. There they should hold fast to the cord of consultation and adopt and enforce that which is conducive to the security, prosperity, wealth and tranquility of the people. For were any measure other than this to be adopted, it could not but result in chaos and commotion.

> (Bahá'u'lláh, *Tablets of Bahá'u'lláh Revealed after the Kitáb-i-Aqdas,* pp. 92–93) [156]

The Great Being saith: The heaven of divine wisdom is illumined with the two luminaries of consultation and compassion. Take ye counsel together in all matters, inasmuch as consultation is the lamp of guidance which leadeth the way, and is the bestower of understanding.

> (Bahá'u'lláh, *Tablets of Bahá'u'lláh Revealed after the Kitáb-i-Aqdas,* p. 168) [157]

If ye travel the countries of the globe ye shall observe on one side the remains of ruin and destruction, while on the other ye shall see the signs of civilization and development. Such desolation and ruin are the result of war, strife and quarreling, while all development and progress are fruits of the lights of virtue, cooperation and concord.

> ('Abdu'l-Bahá, *Selections from the Writings of 'Abdu'l-Bahá,* no. 225.15) [158]

In short, whatsoever thing is arranged in harmony and with love and purity of motive, its result is light, and should the least trace of estrangement prevail the result shall be darkness upon darkness. . . . Discussions must all be confined to spiritual matters that pertain to the training of souls, the instruction of children, the relief of the poor, the help of the feeble throughout all classes in the world, kindness to all peoples, the diffusion of the fragrances of God and the exaltation of His Holy Word.

('Abdu'l-Bahá, cited by Shoghi Effendi in a letter dated 5 March 1922, in *Bahá'í Administration*, p. 22) [159]

Man must consult on all matters, whether major or minor, so that he may become cognizant of what is good. Consultation giveth him insight into things and enableth him to delve into questions which are unknown. The light of truth shineth from the faces of those who engage in consultation. . . . The members who are consulting, however, should behave in the utmost love, harmony and sincerity towards each other. The principle of consultation is one of the most fundamental elements of the divine edifice. Even in their ordinary affairs the individual members of society should consult.

('Abdu'l-Bahá, from a Tablet—translated from the Persian) [160]

Some of the creatures of existence can live solitary and alone. A tree, for instance, may live without the assistance and cooperation of other trees. Some animals are isolated and lead a separate existence away from their kind. But this is impossible for man. In his life and being cooperation and association are essential. Through association and meeting we find happiness and development, individual and collective.

For instance, when there is intercourse and cooperation between two villages, the advancement of each will be assured. Likewise, if intercommunication is established between two cities, both will benefit and progress. And if a reciprocal basis of agreement be reached between two countries, their individual and mutual interests will find great development. . . . It is evident, then, that the outcomes from this basis of agreement and accord are numberless and unlimited.

('Abdu'l-Bahá, *The Promulgation of Universal Peace*, p. 48) [161]

The supreme need of humanity is cooperation and reciprocity. The stronger the ties of fellowship and solidarity amongst men, the greater will be the power of constructiveness and accomplishment in all the planes of human activity. Without cooperation and reciprocal attitude the individual member of human society remains self-centered, uninspired by altruistic purposes, limited and solitary in development like the animal and plant organisms of the lower kingdoms.

('Abdu'l-Bahá, *The Promulgation of Universal Peace*, pp. 478–79)   [162]

The Ancient Beauty, exalted be His Most Great Name, states: "The canopy of world order is upraised upon the two pillars of consultation and compassion," and 'Abdu'l-Bahá in one of His Tablets asserts: "The purpose of consultation is to show that the views of several individuals are assuredly preferable to one man, even as the power of a number of men is of course greater than the power of one man. Thus consultation is acceptable in the presence of the Almighty, and hath been enjoined upon the believers, so that they may confer upon ordinary and personal matters, as well as on affairs which are general in nature and universal. For instance, when a man hath a project to accomplish, should he consult with some of his brethren, that which is agreeable will of course be investigated and unveiled to his eyes, and the truth will be disclosed. Likewise on a higher level, should the people of a village consult one another about their affairs, the right solution will certainly be revealed. In like manner, the members of each profession, such as in industry, should consult, and those in commerce should similarly consult on business affairs. In short, consultation is desirable and acceptable in all things and on all issues."

(Shoghi Effendi, from a letter dated 15 February 1922 written to a Local Spiritual Assembly—translated from the Persian) [163]

The principle of consultation, which constitutes one of the basic laws of the Administration, should be applied to all Bahá'í activities which affect the collective interests of the Faith, for it is through co-operation and continual exchange of thoughts and views that the Cause can best safeguard and foster its interests. Individual initiative, personal ability and resourcefulness, though indispensable, are, unless supported and enriched by the collective experiences and wisdom of the group, utterly incapable of achieving such a tremendous task.

(From a letter dated 30 August 1933 written on behalf of Shoghi Effendi to an individual believer)   [164]

There is nothing that can better ensure the success of your efforts than this close and continued consultation, and he would therefore advise you to adopt this method in all your future activities.

(From a letter dated 30 May 1937 written on behalf of Shoghi Effendi to two believers)   [165]

It is with such thoughts in mind that Bahá'ís enter into collaboration, as their resources permit, with an increasing number of movements, organizations, groups and individuals, establishing partnerships that strive to transform society and further the cause of unity, promote human welfare, and contribute to world solidarity. Indeed, the standard set by passages such as the above inspires the Bahá'í community to become actively engaged in as many aspects of contemporary life as feasible. In choosing areas of collaboration, Bahá'ís are to bear in mind the principle, enshrined in their teachings, that means should be consistent with ends; noble goals cannot be achieved through unworthy means. Specifically, it is not possible to build enduring unity through endeavours that require contention or assume that an inherent conflict of interests underlies all human interactions, however subtly. It should be noted here that, despite the limitations imposed by adherence to this principle, the community has not experienced a shortage of opportunities for collaboration; so many people in the world today are working intensely towards one or another aim which Bahá'ís share. In this respect, they also take care not to overstep certain bounds with their colleagues and associates. They are not to regard any joint undertaking as an occasion to impose religious convictions. Self-righteousness and other unfortunate manifestations of religious zeal are to be utterly avoided. Bahá'ís do, however, readily offer to their collaborators the lessons they have learned through their own experience, just as they are happy to incorporate into their community-building efforts insights gained through such association.

(The Universal House of Justice, from a message dated 2 March 2013 to the Bahá'ís of Iran)   [166]

In their reflections on how to contribute to the betterment of the world, Bahá'ís will undoubtedly recognize that demonstrations are not the only, or even the most effective, means available to them. Rather, they can learn and grow in capacity over time to help their fellow citizens to frame concerns in a way that rises above fissures, to share views in a manner that transcends divisive approaches, and to create and participate in spaces to work together in the quest to enact solutions to the problems that bedevil their nation. As Bahá'u'lláh stated: "Say: no man can attain his true station except through his justice. No power can exist except through unity. No welfare and no well-being can be attained except through consultation." In this light, justice is indeed essential to resist the vain imaginings and idle fancies of social and political machinations, to see reality with one's own eyes, and to identify the requirements for an equitable social order. But then unity is essential—forged through consultative processes, including action and reflection—to achieve the power required for positive social change.

(From a letter dated 27 April 2017 written on behalf of the Universal House of Justice to an individual believer)   [167]

Concepts and principles associated with Bahá'í consultation inform how the friends should interact among themselves and how they participate in social discourses and social action. Consultation provides a means by which common understanding can be reached and a collective course of action defined. It involves a free, respectful, dignified, and fair-minded effort on the part of a group of people to exchange views, seek truth, and attempt to reach consensus. An initial difference of opinion is the starting point for examining an issue in order to reach greater understanding and consensus; it should not become a cause of rancor, aversion, or estrangement. By acting in unity, a conclusion about a particular course of action may be tested and revised as necessary through a process of learning. Otherwise, as 'Abdu'l-Bahá explains, "stubbornness and persistence in one's views will lead ultimately to discord and wrangling and the truth will remain hidden."

(From a letter dated 29 November 2017 written on behalf of the Universal House of Justice to three believers)   [168]

Utilizing Material Means

Hold ye fast unto the cord of material means, placing your whole trust in God, the Provider of all means.

(Bahá'u'lláh, *Tablets of Bahá'u'lláh Revealed after the Kitáb-i-Aqdas*, p. 26)   [169]

In this day it is incumbent upon everyone to serve the Cause of God, while He Who is the Eternal Truth—exalted be His glory—hath made the fulfilment of every undertaking on earth dependent on material means.

(Bahá'u'lláh, from a Tablet—translated from the Persian) [170]

Wealth is praiseworthy in the highest degree, if it is acquired by an individual's own efforts and the grace of God, in commerce, agriculture, art and industry, and if it be expended for philanthropic purposes. Above all, if a judicious and resourceful individual should initiate measures which would universally enrich the masses of the people, there could be no undertaking greater than this, and it would rank in the sight of God as the supreme achievement, for such a benefactor would supply the needs and insure the comfort and well-being of a great multitude. Wealth is most commendable, provided the entire population is wealthy. If, however, a few have inordinate riches while the rest are impoverished, and no fruit or benefit accrues from that wealth, then it is only a liability to its possessor. If, on the other hand, it is expended for the promotion of knowledge, the founding of elementary and other schools, the encouragement of art and industry, the training of orphans and the poor—in brief, if it is dedicated to the welfare of society—its possessor will stand out before God and man as the most excellent of all who live on earth and will be accounted as one of the people of paradise.

('Abdu'l-Bahá, *The Secret of Divine Civilization*, ¶46)   [171]

Thou hast asked about material means and prayer. Prayer is like the spirit and material means are like the human hand. The spirit operateth through the instrumentality of the hand. Although the one true God is the All-Provider, it is the earth which is the means to supply sustenance. "The heaven hath sustenance for you"[4] but when sustenance is decreed it becometh available, whatever the means may be. When man refuseth to use material means, he is like a thirsty one who seeketh to quench his thirst through means other than water or other liquids. The Almighty Lord is the provider of water, and its maker, and hath decreed that it be used to quench man's thirst, but its use is dependent upon His Will. If it should not be in conformity with His Will, man is afflicted with a thirst which the oceans cannot quench.

('Abdu'l-Bahá, from a Tablet—translated from the Persian) [172]

O servant of God! To 'Abdu'l-Bahá, homelessness is home and the gloomy prison his nest. He seeketh a lofty mansion, but in the world of God; he desireth the Frequented Fane, but in the heavenly realm. An earthly edifice, even if raised as high as the heavens, will ultimately become a ruin, nay, a darkened tomb. Erecting edifices, palaces, mansions, and stately homes is acceptable and praiseworthy in the religion of God, but one should not become attached to them or set one's affections upon them. The intention should be the advancement of the world and the establishment of human civilization. A man of true knowledge and understanding will build public structures, that is, places that belong to all—a house of worship, a school to teach children of all ages, a hostel for travellers, a hospital—for every public building is a divine edifice, eternal and everlasting. Upon thee be greetings and praise.

('Abdu'l-Bahá, from a Tablet—translated from the Persian) [173]

Charity, however, does not necessarily imply a project that would fall within the scope of development work; at its simplest, it suggests

4. Qur'án 51:22.

only the transfer of resources, whether financial or of another kind, from those who have plenty to those who have insufficient. The motive that prompts such a benevolent act is, of course, laudable—Bahá'u'lláh Himself declares that "charity is pleasing and praiseworthy in the sight of God and is regarded as a prince among goodly deeds." Nevertheless, the manner in which it is carried out must be carefully considered. It is important, for instance, to avoid any hint of paternalism, and the giver should be conscious of the values implicit in any system of redistribution that he or she establishes.

> (From a letter dated 22 October 2012 written on behalf of the Universal House of Justice to an individual believer)   [174]

The future civilization envisaged by Bahá'u'lláh is a prosperous one, in which the vast resources of the world will be directed towards humanity's elevation and regeneration, not its debasement and destruction. . . . Bahá'ís conduct their lives in the midst of a society acutely disordered in its material affairs. The process of community building they are advancing in their clusters cultivates a set of attitudes towards wealth and possessions very different from those holding sway in the world.

> (The Universal House of Justice, from a message dated 29 December 2015 to the Conference of the Continental Boards of Counsellors)   [175]

The vision of Bahá'u'lláh challenges many of the assumptions that are allowed to shape contemporary discourse—for instance, that self-interest, far from needing to be restrained, drives prosperity, and that progress depends upon its expression through relentless competition. To view the worth of an individual chiefly in terms of how much one can accumulate and how many goods one can consume relative to others is wholly alien to Bahá'í thought. But neither are the teachings in sympathy with sweeping dismissals of wealth as inherently distasteful or immoral, and asceticism is prohibited. Wealth must serve humanity. Its use must accord with spiritual principles; systems must be created in their light. And, in Bahá'u'lláh's memorable words, "No light can compare with the light of justice. The establishment of order in the world and the tranquillity of the nations depend upon it."

(The Universal House of Justice, from a message dated 1 March 2017 to the Bahá'ís of the World)   [176]

SELECTED THEMES PERTAINING TO SOCIAL AND ECONOMIC DEVELOPMENT

Education

Man is the supreme Talisman. Lack of a proper education hath, however, deprived him of that which he doth inherently possess. Through a word proceeding out of the mouth of God he was called into being; by one word more he was guided to recognize the Source of his education; by yet another word his station and destiny were safeguarded. The Great Being saith: Regard man as a mine rich in gems of inestimable value. Education can, alone, cause it to reveal its treasures, and enable mankind to benefit therefrom.

(Bahá'u'lláh, *Tablets of Bahá'u'lláh Revealed after the Kitáb-i-Aqdas*, pp. 161–62) [177]

We prescribe unto all men that which will lead to the exaltation of the Word of God amongst His servants, and likewise, to the advancement of the world of being and the uplift of souls. To this end, the greatest means is education of the child. To this must each and all hold fast. We have verily laid this charge upon you in manifold Tablets as well as in My Most Holy Book. Well is it with him who deferreth thereto.

(Bahá'u'lláh, from a Tablet—translated from the Persian) [178]

Close investigation will show that the primary cause of oppression and injustice, of unrighteousness, irregularity and disorder, is the people's lack of religious faith and the fact that they are uneducated. When, for example, the people are genuinely religious and are literate and well-schooled, and a difficulty presents itself, they can apply to the local authorities; if they do not meet with justice and secure their rights and if they see that the conduct of the local government is incompatible with the divine good pleasure and the king's justice, they can then take their case to higher courts and describe the deviation of the local administration from the spiritual law. Those courts can then send for the local records of the case and in this way justice will be done. At present, however, because of their inadequate schooling, most of the population lack even the vocabulary to explain what they want.

('Abdu'l-Bahá, *The Secret of Divine Civilization*, ¶34)   [179]

The primary, the most urgent requirement is the promotion of education. It is inconceivable that any nation should achieve prosperity and success unless this paramount, this fundamental concern is carried forward. The principal reason for the decline and fall of peoples is ignorance. Today the mass of the people are uninformed even as to ordinary affairs, how much less do they grasp the core of the important problems and complex needs of the time.

('Abdu'l-Bahá, *The Secret of Divine Civilization*, ¶193)   [180]

Observe carefully how education and the arts of civilization bring honor, prosperity, independence and freedom to a government and its people.

It is, furthermore, a vital necessity to establish schools throughout Persia, even in the smallest country towns and villages, and to encourage the people in every possible way to have their children learn to read and write. If necessary, education should even be made compulsory. Until the nerves and arteries of the nation stir into life, every measure that is attempted will prove vain; for the people are as the human body, and determination and the will to struggle are as the soul, and a soulless body does not move. This dynamic power is present to a superlative degree in the very nature of the Persian people, and the spread of education will release it.

('Abdu'l-Bahá, *The Secret of Divine Civilization*, ¶198–99) [181]

And among the teachings of Bahá'u'lláh is the promotion of education. Every child must be instructed in sciences as much as is necessary. If the parents are able to provide the expenses of this education, it is well, otherwise the community must provide the means for the teaching of that child.

('Abdu'l-Bahá, First Tablet to The Hague) [182]

The education and training of children is among the most meritorious acts of humankind and draweth down the grace and favor of the All-Merciful, for education is the indispensable foundation of all human excellence and alloweth man to work his way to the heights of abiding glory.

('Abdu'l-Bahá, *Selections from the Writings of 'Abdu'l-Bahá*, no. 103.1) [183]

It followeth that the children's school must be a place of utmost discipline and order, that instruction must be thorough, and provision must be made for the rectification and refinement of character; so that, in his earliest years, within the very essence of the child, the divine foundation will be laid and the structure of holiness raised up.

('Abdu'l-Bahá, *Selections from the Writings of 'Abdu'l-Bahá*, no. 111.4) [184]

Establish schools that are well organized, and promote the fundamentals of instruction in the various branches of knowledge through teachers who are pure and sanctified, distinguished for their high standards of conduct and general excellence, and strong in faith—scholars and educators with a thorough knowledge of sciences and arts. . . .

Included must be promotion of the arts, the discovery of new wonders, the expansion of trade, and the development of industry. The methods of civilization and the beautification of the country must also be encouraged. . . .

('Abdu'l-Bahá, from a Tablet—translated from the Persian) [185]

One of the friends hath sent us a letter regarding the school at 'Ishqábád, to the effect that, praised be God, the friends there are now working hard to get the school in order, and have appointed teachers well qualified for their task, and that from this time forward the greatest care will be devoted to the supervision and management of the school. . . .

One of the most important of undertakings is the education of children, for success and prosperity depend upon service to and worship of God, the Holy, the All-Glorified.

Among the greatest of all great services is the education of children, and promotion of the various sciences, crafts and arts. Praised be God, ye are now exerting strenuous efforts toward this end. The more ye persevere in this most important task, the more will ye witness the confirmations of God, to such a degree that ye yourselves will be astonished.

('Abdu'l-Bahá, from a Tablet—translated from the Persian) [186]

This school is one of the vital and essential institutions which indeed support and bulwark the edifice of humankind. God willing, it will develop and be perfected along every line. Once this school hath, in every respect, been perfected, once it hath been made to flourish and to surpass all other schools, then, each following the other, more and more schools must be established.

Our meaning is that the friends must direct their attention toward the education and training of all the children of Persia, so that all of them, having, in the school of true learning, achieved the power of understanding and come to know the inner realities of the universe, will go on to uncover the signs and mysteries of God, and will find themselves illumined by the lights of the knowledge of the Lord, and by His love. This truly is the very best way to educate all peoples.

('Abdu'l-Bahá, from a Tablet—translated from the Persian) [187]

Exert every effort to acquire the various branches of knowledge and true understanding. Strain every nerve to achieve both material and spiritual accomplishments.

Encourage the children from their earliest years to master every kind of learning, and make them eager to become skilled in every art—the aim being that through the favouring grace of God, the heart of each one may become even as a mirror disclosing the secrets of the universe, penetrating the innermost reality of all things; and that each may earn world-wide fame in all branches of knowledge, science and the arts.

Certainly, certainly, neglect not the education of the children. Rear them to be possessed of spiritual qualities, and be assured of the gifts and favours of the Lord.

('Abdu'l-Bahá, from a Tablet—translated from the Persian) [188]

Your letter was eloquent, its contents original and sensitively expressed, and it betokened your great and praiseworthy efforts to educate the children, both girls and boys. This is among the most important of all human endeavours. Every possible means of education must be made available to Bahá'í children, tender plants of the divine garden, for in this consisteth the illumination of humankind.

111

Praised be God, the friends in 'Ishqábád have laid a solid foundation, an unassailable base. It was in the City of Love that the first Bahá'í House of Worship was erected; and today in this city the means for the education of children are also being developed, inasmuch as even during the war years this duty was not neglected, and indeed deficiencies were made up for. Now must ye widen the scope of your endeavours and draw up plans to establish schools for higher education, so that the City of Love will become the Bahá'í focal centre for science and the arts. Thanks to the bountiful assistance of the Blessed Beauty, means for this will be provided.

Devote ye particular attention to the school for girls, for the greatness of this wondrous Age will be manifested as a result of progress in the world of women. This is why ye observe that in every land the world of women is on the march, and this is due to the impact of the Most Great Manifestation, and the power of the teachings of God.

Instruction in the schools must begin with instruction in religion. Following religious training, and the binding of the child's heart to the love of God, proceed with his education in the other branches of knowledge.

('Abdu'l-Bahá, from a Tablet—translated from the Persian) [189]

Make ye every effort to improve the Tarbíyat School and to develop order and discipline in this institution. Utilize every means to make this School a garden of the All-Merciful, from which the lights of learning will cast their beams, and wherein the children, whether Bahá'í or other, will be educated to such a degree as to become God's gifts to man, and the pride of the human race. Let them make the greatest progress in the shortest span of time, let them open wide their eyes and uncover the inner realities of all things, become proficient in every art and skill, and learn to comprehend the secrets of all things even as they are—this faculty being one of the clearly evident effects of servitude to the Holy Threshold.

It is certain that ye will make every effort to bring this about, will also draw up plans for the opening of a number of schools. These schools for academic studies must at the same time be training centres in behaviour and conduct, and they must favour character and conduct above the sciences and arts. Good behaviour and high moral character must come first, for unless the character be trained, acquiring knowledge will only prove injurious. Knowledge is praiseworthy when it is coupled with ethical conduct and virtuous character; otherwise it is a deadly poison, a frightful danger. A physician of evil character, and who betrayeth his trust, can bring on death, and become the source of numerous infirmities and diseases.

Devote ye the utmost attention to this matter, for the basic, the foundation-principle of a school is first and foremost moral training, character and the rectification of conduct.

('Abdu'l-Bahá, from a Tablet—translated from the Persian) [190]

The subjects to be taught in children's schools are many, and for lack of time We can touch on only a few: First and most important is training in behaviour and good character; the rectification of qualities; arousing the desire to become accomplished and acquire perfections, and to cleave unto the religion of God and stand firm in His Laws: to accord total obedience to every just government, to show forth loyalty and trustworthiness to the ruler of the time, to be well wishers of mankind, to be kind to all.

And further, as well as in the ideals of character, instruction in such arts and sciences as are of benefit, and in foreign tongues. Also, the repeating of prayers for the well-being of ruler and ruled; and the avoidance of materialistic works that are current among those who see only natural causation, and tales of love, and books that arouse the passions.

To sum up, let all the lessons be entirely devoted to the acquisition of human perfections.

Here, then, in brief are directions for the curriculum of these schools.

('Abdu'l-Bahá, from a Tablet—translated from the Persian) [191]

Your letter hath come and hath occasioned the utmost joy, with its news that, praised be God, in Hamadán a welfare and relief association hath been established. I trust that this will become a source of general prosperity and assistance, and that means will be provided to set the hearts of the poor and weak at rest, and to educate the orphans and other children.

The question of training the children and looking after the orphans is extremely important, but most important of all is the education of girl children, for these girls will one day be mothers, and the mother is the first teacher of the child. In whatever way she reareth the child, so will the child become, and the results of that first training will remain with the individual throughout his entire life, and it would be most difficult to alter them. And how can a mother, herself ignorant and untrained, educate her child? It is therefore clear that the education of girls is of far greater consequence than that of boys. This fact is extremely important, and the matter must be seen to with the greatest energy and dedication.

God sayeth in the Qur'án that they shall not be equals, those who have knowledge and those who have it not.[5] Ignorance is thus utterly to be blamed, whether in male or female; indeed, in the female its harm is greater. I hope, therefore, that the friends will make strenuous efforts

5. Qur'án 39:12.

to educate their children, sons and daughters alike. This is verily the truth, and outside the truth there is manifestly naught save perdition.

('Abdu'l-Bahá, from a Tablet—translated from the Arabic and Persian) [192]

In this new and wondrous Cause, the advancement of all branches of knowledge is a fixed and vital principle, and the friends, one and all, are obligated to make every effort toward this end, so that the Cause of the Manifest Light may be spread abroad, and that every child, according to his need, will receive his share of the sciences and arts— until not even a single peasant's child will be found who is completely devoid of schooling.

It is essential that the fundamentals of knowledge be taught; essential that all should be able to read and write. Wherefore is this new institution most worthy of praise, and its programme to be encouraged. The hope is that other villages will take you for a model, and that in every village where there is a certain number of believers, a school will be founded where the children can study reading, writing, and basic knowledge.

('Abdu'l-Bahá, from a Tablet—translated from the Persian) [193]

Bahá'u'lláh has announced that inasmuch as ignorance and lack of education are barriers of separation among mankind, all must receive training and instruction. Through this provision the lack of mutual understanding will be remedied and the unity of mankind furthered and advanced. Universal education is a universal law.

('Abdu'l-Baha, *The Promulgation of Universal Peace*, p. 417) [194]

Among the sacred obligations devolving upon the Spiritual Assemblies is the promotion of learning, the establishing of schools and creation of the necessary academic equipment and facilities for every boy and girl.

115

Every child, without exception, must from his earliest years make a thorough study of the art of reading and writing, and according to his own tastes and inclinations and the degree of his capacity and powers, devote extreme diligence to the acquisition of learning beneficial arts and skills, various languages, speech, and contemporary technology.

To assist the children of the poor in the attainment of these accomplishments, and particularly in learning the basic subjects, is incumbent upon the members of the Spiritual Assemblies, and is accounted as one of the obligations laid upon the conscience of the trustees of God in every land.

"He that bringeth up his son or the son of another, it is as though he hath brought up a son of Mine; upon him rest My Glory, My Loving-Kindness, My Mercy, that have compassed the world."

(Shoghi Effendi, from a letter dated 8 June 1925 written to the Spiritual Assemblies of the East—translated from the Persian) [195]

You had asked about poverty and wealth, and the toil of the poor and the comfort of the rich, and you had expressed your amazement and wonder at this situation. . . .

The intent is not, however, to say that all the poor will become rich and they will become equal. Such a concept is like saying that all the ignorant and the illiterate will become the sages of the age and the learned of the learned. Rather, when education becomes compulsory and universal, ignorance and illiteracy will decrease and there will remain no one deprived of education. But, as the basis for distinction is in the person's capacity and ability, and differences are related to the degree of his intelligence and mental powers, therefore, all the people will not be equal in their knowledge, learning and understanding. The intent is to say that the world of creation calls for distinctions in people's stations, and degrees in the differences existing among them, so that the affairs of the world may become organized and ordered. Diversity in all created things, whether in kind, in physical appearance, or in station, is the means for their protection, their permanence, unity and harmony. Each part complements the other.

(From a letter dated 22 May 1928 written on behalf of Shoghi Effendi to an individual believer—translated from the Persian) [196]

. . . Bahá'u'lláh considered education as one of the most fundamental factors of a true civilization. This education, however, in order to be adequate and fruitful, should be comprehensive in nature and should take into consideration not only the physical and the intellectual side of man but also his spiritual and ethical aspects.

(From a letter dated 9 July 1931 written on behalf of Shoghi Effendi to an individual believer) [197]

You have asked him for detailed information concerning the Bahá'í educational programme. There is as yet no such thing as a Bahá'í curriculum, and there are no Bahá'í publications exclusively devoted to this subject, since the teachings of Bahá'u'lláh and 'Abdu'l-Bahá do not present a definite and detailed educational system, but simply offer certain basic principles and set forth a number of teaching ideals that should guide future Bahá'í educationalists in their efforts to formulate an adequate teaching curriculum which would be in full harmony with the spirit of the Bahá'í Teachings, and would thus meet the requirements and needs of the modern age.

These basic principles are available in the sacred writings of the Cause, and should be carefully studied, and gradually incorporated in various college and university programmes. But the task of formulating a system of education which would be officially recognized by the Cause, and enforced as such throughout the Bahá'í world, is one which

[the] present-day generation of believers cannot obviously undertake, and which has to be gradually accomplished by Bahá'í scholars and educationalists of the future.

(From a letter dated 7 June 1939 written on behalf of Shoghi Effendi to an individual believer)   [198]

Education is a vast field, and educational theories abound. Surely many have considerable merit, but it should be remembered that none is free of assumptions about the nature of the human being and society. An educational process should, for example, create in a child awareness of his or her potentialities, but the glorification of self has to be scrupulously avoided. So often in the name of building confidence the ego is bolstered. Similarly, play has its place in the education of the young. Children and junior youth, however, have proven time and again their capacity to engage in discussions on abstract subjects, undertaken at a level appropriate to their age, and derive great joy from the serious pursuit of understanding. An educational process that dilutes content in a mesmerizing sea of entertainment does them no service.

(The Universal House of Justice, from a message dated 12 December 2011 to all National Spiritual Assemblies) [199]

Agriculture

Whilst in the Prison of 'Akká, We revealed in the Crimson Book that which is conducive to the advancement of mankind and to the reconstruction of the world. The utterances set forth therein by the Pen of the Lord of creation include the following which constitute the fundamental principles for the administration of the affairs of men:

First: It is incumbent upon the ministers of the House of Justice to promote the Lesser Peace so that the people of the earth may be relieved from the burden of exorbitant expenditures. This matter is imperative and absolutely essential, inasmuch as hostilities and conflict lie at the root of affliction and calamity.

Second: Languages must be reduced to one common language to be taught in all the schools of the world.

Third: It behooveth man to adhere tenaciously unto that which will promote fellowship, kindliness and unity.

Fourth: Everyone, whether man or woman, should hand over to a trusted person a portion of what he or she earneth through trade, agriculture or other occupation, for the training and education of children, to be spent for this purpose with the knowledge of the Trustees of the House of Justice.

Fifth: Special regard must be paid to agriculture. Although it hath been mentioned in the fifth place, unquestionably it precedeth the others.

> (Bahá'u'lláh, *Tablets of Bahá'u'lláh Revealed after the Kitáb-i-Aqdas*, pp. 89–90)   [200]

Thou hadst made reference in thy letter to agriculture. On this matter He hath laid down the following universal rule that it is incumbent upon everyone, even should he be resident in a particular land for no more than a single day, to become engaged in some craft or trade, or agriculture, and that the very pursuit of such a calling is, in the eyes of the one true God, identical with worship. This rule was exemplified by the Bahá'í community at the time when they were facing exile from 'Iráq, for, while they were making arrangements for their journey, they occupied themselves in cultivating the land; and when they set out, instructions were given for the fruits of their labours to be distributed amongst the friends.

> (Bahá'u'lláh, from a Tablet—translated from the Persian)
> [201]

And if, as you pass by fields and plantations, where the plants, flowers and sweet-smelling herbs are growing luxuriantly together, forming a pattern of unity, this is an evidence of the fact that that plantation and garden is flourishing under the care of a skilful gardener. But when you see it in a state of disorder and irregularity you infer that it has lacked the training of an efficient farmer and thus has produced weeds and tares.

('Abdu'l-Bahá, First Tablet to The Hague) [202]

Strive as much as possible to become proficient in the science of agriculture, for in accordance with the divine teachings the acquisition of sciences and the perfection of arts are considered acts of worship. If a man engageth with all his power in the acquisition of a science or in the perfection of an art, it is as if he has been worshiping God in churches and temples. Thus as thou enterest a school of agriculture and strivest in the acquisition of that science thou art day and night engaged in acts of worship—acts that are accepted at the threshold of the Almighty. What bounty greater than this, that science should be considered as an act of worship and art as service to the Kingdom of God.

('Abdu'l-Bahá, *Selections from the Writings of 'Abdu'l-Bahá*, no. 126.1) [203]

Since thy dear child is taking his examinations, my fervent wish at the divine Threshold is that, by the grace and favour of God, he may meet with success, and that in the future he may go on to study agriculture and master its various branches, practical and theoretical. Agriculture is a noble science and, should thy son become proficient in this field, he will become a means of providing for the comfort of untold numbers of people.

('Abdu'l-Bahá, from a Tablet—translated from the Persian) [204]

Commerce, agriculture and industry should not, in truth, be a bar to service of the one true God. Indeed, such occupations are most potent instruments and clear proofs for the manifestation of the evidences of one's piety, of one's trustworthiness and of the virtues of the All-Merciful Lord.

('Abdu'l-Bahá, from a Tablet—translated from the Persian) [205]

The crisis that exists in the world is not confined to the farmers. Its effects have reached every means of livelihood. The farmers are in a sense better off because they at least have food to eat. But on the whole the crisis is serving a great purpose. It is broadening the outlook of man, teaching him to think internationally, forcing him to take into consideration the welfare of his neighbours if he wishes to improve his own condition.

(From a letter dated 2 March 1932 written on behalf of Shoghi Effendi to an individual believer) [206]

Economics

O My Servants! Ye are the trees of My garden; ye must give forth goodly and wondrous fruits, that ye yourselves and others may profit therefrom. Thus it is incumbent on every one to engage in crafts and professions, for therein lies the secret of wealth, O men of understanding! For results depend upon means, and the grace of God shall be all-sufficient unto you. Trees that yield no fruit have been and will ever be for the fire.

(Bahá'u'lláh, The Hidden Words, Persian, no. 80) [207]

Should these sublime teachings be diffused, mankind shall be freed from all perils, from all chronic ills and sicknesses. In like manner are

SOCIAL ACTION

the Bahá'í economic principles the embodiment of the highest aspirations of all wage-earning classes and of economists of various schools.

('Abdu'l-Bahá, Tablet to Dr. Forel)   [208]

To state the matter briefly, the Teachings of Bahá'u'lláh advocate voluntary sharing, and this is a greater thing than the equalization of wealth. For equalization must be imposed from without, while sharing is a matter of free choice.

Man reacheth perfection through good deeds, voluntarily performed, not through good deeds the doing of which was forced upon him. And sharing is a personally chosen righteous act: that is, the rich should extend assistance to the poor, they should expend their substance for the poor, but of their own free will, and not because the poor have gained this end by force. For the harvest of force is turmoil and the ruin of the social order. On the other hand voluntary sharing, the freely-chosen expending of one's substance, leadeth to society's comfort and peace. It lighteth up the world; it bestoweth honor upon humankind.

('Abdu'l-Bahá, *Selections from the Writings of 'Abdu'l-Bahá*, no. 79.2–3)   [209]

O my spiritual friends! Among the greatest means of achieving modern advancements, the prosperity of nations, and the civilization of the peoples is the establishment of companies for commerce, industry, and other sources of wealth, inasmuch as a company is a symbol of oneness, unity, and harmony in the Cause of God. It is most difficult for humankind to succeed in anything singly, but when an assemblage is formed and a company established, the members will be enabled jointly to accomplish great tasks. Consider, for instance, an army. If each soldier were to enter into combat singly, he would be fighting with the force of one man, but when a troop is formed, each member of that troop resisteth with a thousand-fold power, for the power of a thousand individuals is converged upon one point. It is the same in other matters. However, every business company should be established on divine principles. Its foundations should be trustworthiness, piety, and truthfulness, in order to protect the rights of the people and to become, as day followeth day, a magnet of fidelity, so that the confirmations of the All-Glorious may be unveiled. Moreover, a legitimate company must needs exert all within its power to safeguard the rights of the people in all matters, whether great or small, and to administer the affairs of the company with the utmost perfection, uprightness, and care. If it be so conducted, that company, beyond a shadow of a doubt, will become the embodiment of blessings, and that assemblage will attract the confirmations of the Lord of all bounties and, safe under the protection of the Greatest Name, will remain shielded from every misfortune. Upon you be greetings and praise.

('Abdu'l-Bahá, from a Tablet—translated from the Persian) [210]

The question of economics must commence with the farmer and then be extended to the other classes inasmuch as the number of farmers is far greater than all other classes. Therefore, it is fitting to begin with the farmer in matters related to economics for the farmer is the first active agent in human society. In brief, from among the wise men in every village a board should be set up and the affairs of that village should be under the control of that board. Likewise a general storehouse should be founded with the appointment of a secretary. At the time of the harvest, under the direction of that board, a certain percentage of the entire harvest should be appropriated for the storehouse.

The storehouse has seven revenues: Tithes, taxes on animals, property without an heir, all lost objects found whose owners cannot be traced, one third of all treasure-trove, one third of the produce of all mines, and voluntary contributions.

This storehouse also has seven expenditures:

1. General running expenses of the storehouse, such as the salary of the secretary and the administration of public health.

2. Tithes to the government.

3. Taxes on animals to the government.

4. Costs of running an orphanage.

5. Costs of running a home for the incapacitated.

6. Costs of running a school.

7. Payment of subsidies to provide needed support of the poor.

The first revenue is the tithe. It should be collected as follows: If, for instance, the income of a person is five hundred dollars and his necessary expenses are the same, no tithes will be collected from him. If another's expenses are five hundred dollars while his income is one thousand dollars, one tenth will be taken from him, for he hath more than his needs; if he giveth one tenth of the surplus, his livelihood will not be adversely affected. If another's expenses are one thousand dollars, and his income is five thousand dollars, as he hath four thousand dollars surplus he will be required to give one and a half tenths. If another person hath necessary expenses of one thousand dollars, but his income is ten thousand dollars, from him two tenths will be required for his surplus represents a large sum. But if the necessary expenses of another person are four or five thousand dollars, and his income one hundred thousand, one fourth will be required from him. On the other hand, should a person's income be two hundred, but his needs absolutely essential for his livelihood be five hundred dollars, and provided he hath not been remiss in his work or his farm hath not been blessed with a harvest, such a one must receive help from the general storehouse so that he may not remain in need and may live in comfort.

A certain amount must be put aside from the general storehouse for the orphans of the village and a certain sum for the incapacitated. A certain amount must be provided from this storehouse for those who are needy and incapable of earning a livelihood, and a certain amount for the village's system of education. And, a certain amount must be set aside for the administration of public health. If anything is left in the storehouse, that must be transferred to the general treasury of the nation for national expenditures.

('Abdu'l-Bahá, from a Tablet—translated from the Persian) [211]

One must therefore enact such laws and regulations as will moderate the excessive fortunes of the few and meet the basic needs of the myriad millions of the poor, that a degree of moderation may be achieved.

However, absolute equality is just as untenable, for complete equality in wealth, power, commerce, agriculture, and industry would result in chaos and disorder, disrupt livelihoods, provoke universal discontent, and undermine the orderly conduct of the affairs of the community. For unjustified equality is also fraught with peril. It is preferable, then, that some measure of moderation be achieved, and by moderation is meant the enactment of such laws and regulations as would prevent the unwarranted concentration of wealth in the hands of the few and satisfy the essential needs of the many. For instance, the factory owners reap a fortune every day, but the wage the poor workers are paid cannot even meet their daily needs: This is most unfair, and assuredly no just man can accept it. Therefore, laws and regulations should be enacted which would grant the workers both a daily wage and a share in a fourth or fifth of the profits of the factory in accordance with its means, or which would have the workers equitably share in some other way in the profits with the owners. For the capital and the management come from the latter and the toil and labour from the former. The workers could either be granted a wage that adequately meets their daily needs, as well as a right to a share in the revenues of the factory when they are injured, incapacitated, or unable to work, or else a wage could be set that allows the workers to both satisfy their daily needs and save a little for times of weakness and incapacity.

If matters were so arranged, neither would the factory owners amass each day a fortune which is absolutely of no use to them—for should one's fortune increase beyond measure, one would come under a most heavy burden, become subject to exceeding hardships and troubles, and find the administration of such an excessive fortune to be most difficult and to exhaust one's natural powers—nor would the workers endure such toil and hardship as to become incapacitated and to fall victim, at the end of their lives, to the direst need.

It is therefore clearly established that the appropriation of excessive wealth by a few individuals, notwithstanding the needs of the masses, is unfair and unjust, and that, conversely, absolute equality would also disrupt the existence, welfare, comfort, peace, and orderly life of the human race. Such being the case, the best course is therefore to seek moderation, which is for the wealthy to recognize the advantages of moderation in the acquisition of profits and to show regard for the welfare of the poor and the needy, that is, to fix a daily wage for the workers and also to allot them a share of the total profits of the factory.

('Abdu'l-Bahá, *Some Answered Questions*, no. 78.4–7)   [212]

Among the results of the manifestation of spiritual forces will be that the human world will adapt itself to a new social form, the justice of God will become manifest throughout human affairs, and human equality will be universally established. The poor will receive a great bestowal, and the rich attain eternal happiness. For although at the present time the rich enjoy the greatest luxury and comfort, they are nevertheless deprived of eternal happiness; for eternal happiness is contingent upon giving, and the poor are everywhere in the state of abject need. Through the manifestation of God's great equity the poor of the world will be rewarded and assisted fully, and there will be a readjustment in the economic conditions of mankind so that in the future there will not be the abnormally rich nor the abject poor. The rich will enjoy the privilege of this new economic condition as well as the poor, for owing to certain provisions and restrictions they will not be able to accumulate so much as to be burdened by its management, while the poor will be relieved from the stress of want and misery. The rich will enjoy his palace, and the poor will have his comfortable cottage.

('Abdu'l-Bahá, *The Promulgation of Universal Peace*, pp. 182–83) [213]

. . . Bahá'u'lláh set forth principles of guidance and teaching for economic readjustment. Regulations were revealed by Him which ensure the welfare of the commonwealth. As the rich man enjoys his life surrounded by ease and luxuries, so the poor man must, likewise, have a home and be provided with sustenance and comforts commensurate with his needs. This readjustment of the social economy is of the greatest importance inasmuch as it ensures the stability of the world of humanity; and until it is effected, happiness and prosperity are impossible.

('Abdu'l-Bahá, *The Promulgation of Universal Peace*, p. 252) [214]

One of Bahá'u'lláh's teachings is the adjustment of means of livelihood in human society. Under this adjustment there can be no extremes in human conditions as regards wealth and sustenance. For the community needs financier, farmer, merchant and laborer just as an army must be composed of commander, officers and privates. All cannot be commanders; all cannot be officers or privates. Each in his station in the social fabric must be competent—each in his function according to ability but with justness of opportunity for all. . . .

Difference of capacity in human individuals is fundamental. It is impossible for all to be alike, all to be equal, all to be wise. Bahá'u'lláh has revealed principles and laws which will accomplish the adjustment of varying human capacities. He has said that whatsoever is possible of accomplishment in human government will be effected through these principles. When the laws He has instituted are carried out, there will be no millionaires possible in the community and likewise no extremely poor. This will be effected and regulated by adjusting the different degrees of human capacity. The fundamental basis of the community is agriculture, tillage of the soil. All must be producers. Each person in the community whose need is equal to his individual producing capacity shall be exempt from taxation. But if his income is greater than his needs, he must pay a tax until an adjustment is effected. That is to say, a man's capacity for production and his needs will be equalized and reconciled through taxation. If his production exceeds, he will pay a tax; if his necessities exceed his production, he shall receive an amount sufficient to equalize or adjust. Therefore, taxation will be proportionate to capacity and production, and there will be no poor in the community.

('Abdu'l-Bahá, *The Promulgation of Universal Peace*, pp. 301–3)
[215]

The fundamentals of the whole economic condition are divine in nature and are associated with the world of the heart and spirit. This is fully explained in the Bahá'í teaching, and without knowledge of its principles no improvement in the economic state can be realized. The Bahá'ís will bring about this improvement and betterment but not through sedition and appeal to physical force—not through warfare, but welfare. Hearts must be so cemented together, love must become so dominant that the rich shall most willingly extend assistance to the poor and take steps to establish these economic adjustments permanently. If it is accomplished in this way, it will be most praiseworthy because then it will be for the sake of God and in the pathway of His service. For example, it will be as if the rich inhabitants of a city should say, "It is neither just nor lawful that we should possess great wealth while there is abject poverty in this community," and then willingly give their wealth to the poor, retaining only as much as will enable them to live comfortably.

('Abdu'l-Bahá, *The Promulgation of Universal Peace*, p. 334)

[216]

He has also received the article you wrote for "The Bahá'í World" on the economic teachings of the Cause.[6] As you say, the writings are not so rich on this subject, and many of the issues at present baffling the minds of the world are not even mentioned. The primary consideration is the spirit that has to permeate our economic life and this will gradually crystallize itself into definite institutions and principles that would help to bring about the ideal condition foretold by Bahá'u'lláh.

(From a letter dated 20 December 1931 written on behalf of Shoghi Effendi to a National Spiritual Assembly)   [217]

With regard to your wish for reorganizing your business along Bahá'í lines, Shoghi Effendi deeply appreciates the spirit that has prompted you to make such a suggestion. But he feels, nevertheless, that the time has not yet come for any believer to bring about such a fundamental change in the economic structure of our society, however restricted may be the field for such an experiment. The economic teachings of the Cause, though well known in their main outline, have not yet been

---

6. "The World Economy of Bahá'u'lláh" by Horace Holley, in *The Bahá'í World*, vol. 4, 1930–1932 (New York: Bahá'í Publishing Committee, 1933), pp. 351–67.

sufficiently elaborated and systematized to allow anyone to make an exact and thorough application of them, even on a restricted scale.

(From a letter dated 22 May 1935 written on behalf of Shoghi Effendi to an individual believer)   [218]

There are practically no <u>technical</u> teachings on economics in the Cause, such as banking, the price system, and others. The Cause is not an economic system, nor should its Founders be considered as having been <u>technical</u> economists. The contribution of the Faith to this subject is essentially indirect, as it consists in the application of spiritual principles to our present-day economic system. Bahá'u'lláh has given us a few basic principles which should guide future Bahá'í economists in establishing such institutions as will adjust the economic relationships of the world.

. . . The Master has definitely stated that wages should be unequal, simply because men are unequal in their ability, and hence should receive wages that would correspond to their varying capacities and resources. This view seems to contradict the opinion of some modern economists. But the friends should have full confidence in the words of the Master, and should give preference to His statements over those voiced by our so-called modern thinkers. . . .

. . . Whatever the progress of the machinery may be, man will have always to toil in order to earn his living. Effort is an inseparable part of man's life. It may take different forms with the changing conditions of the world, but it will be always present as a necessary element in our earthly existence. Life is after all a struggle. Progress is attained through struggle, and without such a struggle life ceases to have a meaning; it becomes even extinct. The progress of machinery has not made effort unnecessary. It has given it a new form, a new outlet.

. . . By the statement "the economic solution is divine in nature" is meant that religion alone can, in the last resort, bring in man's nature such a fundamental change as to enable him to adjust the economic relationships of society. It is only in this way that man can control the economic forces that threaten to disrupt the foundations of his existence, and thus assert his mastery over the forces of nature.

. . . As already referred to . . . , social inequality is the inevitable outcome of the natural inequality of men. Human beings are different in ability and should, therefore, be different in their social and economic standing. Extremes of wealth and poverty should, however, be totally abolished. Those whose brains have contributed to the creation and improvement of the means of production must be fairly rewarded, though these means may be owned and controlled by others.

(From a letter dated 26 December 1935 written on behalf of Shoghi Effendi to an individual believer) [219]

With regard to your question concerning the Bahá'í attitude towards labour problems: these cannot assuredly be solved, 'Abdu'l-Bahá tells us, through the sheer force of physical violence. Non-co-operation too, even though not accompanied by acts of violence, is ineffective. The conflict between labour and capital can best be solved through the peaceful and constructive methods of co-operation and of consultation.

(From a letter dated 30 June 1937 written on behalf of Shoghi Effendi to an individual believer) [220]

Regarding your questions concerning the Bahá'í attitude on various economic problems, such as the problem of ownership, control and distribution of capital, and of other means of production, the problem of trusts and monopolies, and such economic experiments as social co-operatives: the Teachings of Bahá'u'lláh and 'Abdu'l-Bahá do not provide specific and detailed solutions to all such economic questions, which mostly pertain to the domain of technical economics, and as such do not concern directly the Cause. True, there are certain guiding principles in Bahá'í Sacred Writings on the subject of economics, but these do by no means cover the whole field of theoretical and applied economics, and are mostly intended to guide future Bahá'í economic writers and technicians to evolve an economic system which would function in full conformity with the spirit, and the exact provisions of the Cause on this and similar subjects. The International House of Justice will have, in consultation with economic experts, to assist in the formulation and evolution of the Bahá'í economic system of the future. One thing, however, is certain: that the Cause neither accepts the theories of the Capitalistic economics in full, nor can it agree with the Marxists and Communists in their repudiation of the principle of private ownership and of this vital sacred right of the individual.

(From a letter dated 10 June 1939 written on behalf of Shoghi Effendi to an individual believer)   [221]

The ideologies now current in the world are extremely complex. Just as it is difficult to identify any longer a coherent system of teachings which could be called Christianity and embrace all those who call themselves Christians, so there are many kinds of Communist, often stridently at variance with one another. Even more so are there many kinds of "Capitalist" in the sense of those who advocate Capitalism as the most desirable form of economic system. "The Promise of World Peace" was no place for an analysis of the virtues and shortcomings of these various theories, it could but allude to some of the most glaring deficiencies produced by extreme variants, and encourage all who advocate them to overlook their differences in a search for the real solution of the problems afflicting mankind.

One could postulate two extremes of economic theory: those who believe that the best solution is to remove all governmental control and intervention from the operation of the economic system, and those who believe that the functioning of the economic system should be closely supervised and adjusted by the State so that society is not at the mercy of the system but has it under its control. As has become abundantly clear, neither extreme is workable, and proponents of both have gradually come to adopt more moderate stances, although there tends to be an oscillation of viewpoints in response to changing conditions. It was to the proponents of one of these extremes and to the current highly unsatisfactory economic situation in the world that the House of Justice was alluding when it referred to those ideologies which have tended "to callously abandon starving millions to the operations of a market system that all too clearly is aggravating the plight of the majority of mankind, while enabling small sections to live in a condition of affluence scarcely dreamed of by our forebears."

(From a letter dated 13 November 1985 written on behalf of the Universal House of Justice to an individual believer) [222]

An obvious example arises in discussions of the process of globalization, to which your letter alludes. The immense advantages, that this long-awaited stage in the evolution of human society brings with it, demand of government and civil society comparable efforts to ensure a fair distribution of its benefits to the whole of humankind. 'Abdu'l-Bahá sets the issue squarely before us:

Consider an individual who has amassed treasures by colonizing a country for his profit: he has obtained an incomparable fortune and has secured profits and incomes which flow like a river, while a hundred thousand unfortunate people, weak and powerless, are in need of a mouthful of bread. There is neither equality nor benevolence. So you see that general peace and joy are destroyed, and the welfare of humanity is negated to such an extent as to make fruitless the lives of many. For fortune, honours, commerce, industry are in the hands of some industrialists, while other people are submitted to quite a series of difficulties and to limitless troubles: they have neither advantages, nor profits, nor comforts, nor peace.

The challenges posed by this issue, which today affects the whole planet, are on a scale unprecedented in human history. Addressing them will require unity of understanding about what is at stake, an understanding that can be achieved only by searching analysis, open public discussion and an unrelenting commitment to putting into effect agreed upon systems of control.

(From a letter dated 27 November 2001 written on behalf of the Universal House of Justice to an individual believer) [223]

The Universal House of Justice has received your letter . . . requesting clarification on what constitutes an appropriate economic philosophy for our time. . . .

In your . . . letter you quote a passage from *Century of Light*, which refers to the current reigning system of thought on the planet as morally and intellectually bankrupt. The passage suggests to you that capitalism is regarded by the Bahá'í community as a useless economic philosophy for future world development. You find this stance surprising not only because it is in direct opposition to conclusions reached by thinkers today who consider capitalism the only viable system for global economic development, but also because it seems to contradict certain statements made by Shoghi Effendi. Capitalism has evolved into a system which you would argue is largely, if not entirely, consistent with Shoghi Effendi's statements. You wonder how Bahá'ís working in the field of economics are to move forward, when they hold such widely differing views on the subject, from those like you who see the Guardian's remarks as support for capitalism to others who believe it should be replaced.

There are two aspects to the questions you raise. One concerns the statement about the moral bankruptcy of today's dominant world system, and the other is related to the validity of economic theories that embrace capitalism. As to the first, the passage you quote from *Century of Light* is intended as a general statement on the condition of the world, its political and economic structures, and the injustices that are tearing away the fabric of present-day society. One can rightly denounce as unjust the current global situation, in which a relatively few live in opulence while the vast majority of their fellow human beings are condemned to a life of utter material poverty. Surely this situation cannot be separated from the basic inadequacies of the dominant system of thought and the structures and processes to which it has given rise.

The second aspect of your questions concerns the specifics of economic theory. That, as you mention, Bahá'í thinkers adhere to a wide range of views on capitalism and its various forms should not be a cause for alarm. On the contrary, the House of Justice finds the situation quite healthy and does not wish to elaborate further on the subject at this time. You are correct when you make the statement in your . . . letter that the solutions to humanity's problems are to be found in the application of scientific knowledge and the Teachings of Bahá'u'lláh to social reality. It is to be expected, then, that the Teachings would be brought to bear on the choices humanity has to make about how to produce, distribute, multiply, apply and use material means. As is natural in the advancement of any science, insights into a proper economic theory will only be gained as people with divergent views explore different directions. Criticism of current economic practices should not be misconstrued as simply a denunciation of capitalism, nor should it be taken as an endorsement of socialism. As you would readily agree, the premise of private ownership can give rise to new and better ways than current modes of organizing the economic activity of the human race.

(From a letter dated 31 July 2002 written on behalf of the Universal House of Justice to an individual believer)   [224]

Social justice will be attained only when every member of society enjoys a relative degree of material prosperity and gives due regard to the acquisition of spiritual qualities. The solution, then, to prevailing economic difficulties is to be sought as much in the application of spiritual principles as in the implementation of scientific methods and approaches. The family unit offers an ideal setting within which can be shaped those moral attributes that contribute to an appropriate view of material wealth and its utilization.

Referring to the exigencies of the material world, Bahá'u'lláh has affirmed that to every end has been assigned a means for its accomplishment. A natural conclusion to be drawn from reflection on this fundamental principle is that vigilance must be exercised in distinguishing "means" from "ends"; otherwise, what is intended as a mere instrument could easily become the very goal of an individual's life. The acquisition of wealth is a case in point; it is acceptable and praiseworthy to the extent that it serves as a means for achieving higher ends—for meeting one's basic necessities, for fostering the progress of one's family, for promoting the welfare of society, and for contributing to the establishment of a world civilization. But to make the accumulation of wealth the central purpose of one's life is unworthy of any human being.

An idea closely related to the above, and well in accord with the spirit of the Bahá'í teachings, is that the end does not serve to justify the means. However constructive and noble the goal, however significant to one's life or to the welfare of one's family, it must not be attained through improper means. Regrettably, a number of today's leaders—political, social, and religious—as well as some of the directors of financial markets, executives of multinational corporations, chiefs of commerce and industry, and ordinary people who succumb to social pressure and ignore the call of their conscience, act against this principle; they justify any means in order to achieve their goals.

The legitimacy of wealth depends, 'Abdu'l-Bahá has indicated, on how it is acquired and on how it is expended. In this connection, He has stated that "wealth is praiseworthy in the highest degree, if it is acquired by an individual's own efforts and the grace of God, in commerce, agriculture, crafts and industry," if the measures adopted by the individual in generating wealth serve to "enrich the generality of the people," and if the wealth thus obtained is expended for "philanthropic purposes" and "the promotion of knowledge," for the establishment of schools and industry and the advancement of education, and in general for the welfare of society. . . .

Many would readily acknowledge that the acquisition of wealth should be governed by the requirements of justice, which, as a principle, can be expressed to varying degrees, on different levels. An employer and employee, for example, are bound by the laws and conventions that regulate their work, and each is expected to carry out his or her responsibilities with honesty and integrity. At another level, however, if the deeper implications of justice are to be realized, the other two preconditions to the legitimate acquisition of wealth mentioned above must be taken into account, and prevailing norms reassessed in their light. Here, the relationship between minimum wage and the cost of living merits careful evaluation—this, especially in light of the contribution workers make to a company's success and their entitlement, as noted by 'Abdu'l-Bahá, to a fair share of the profits. The wide margin, often unjustifiable, between the production costs of certain goods and the price at which they are sold likewise requires attention, as does the question of the generation of wealth through measures that "enrich the generality of the people," What such reflection and inquiry will no doubt make abundantly clear is that certain approaches to obtaining wealth—so many of which involve the exploitation of others, the monopolization and manipulation of markets, and the production of goods that promote violence and immorality—are unworthy and unacceptable.

(The Universal House of Justice, from a message dated 2 April 2010 to the Believers in the Cradle of the Faith)   [225]

The welfare of any segment of humanity is inextricably bound up with the welfare of the whole. Humanity's collective life suffers when any one group thinks of its own well-being in isolation from that of its neighbours or pursues economic gain without regard for how the natural environment, which provides sustenance for all, is affected. A stubborn obstruction, then, stands in the way of meaningful social progress: time and again, avarice and self-interest prevail at the expense of the common good. Unconscionable quantities of wealth are being amassed, and the instability this creates is made worse by how income and opportunity are spread so unevenly both between nations and within nations. But it need not be so. However much such conditions are the outcome of history, they do not have to define the future, and even if current approaches to economic life satisfied humanity's stage of adolescence, they are certainly inadequate for its dawning age of maturity. There is no justification for continuing to perpetuate structures, rules, and systems that manifestly fail to serve the interests of all peoples. The teachings of the Faith leave no room for doubt: there is an inherent moral dimension to the generation, distribution, and utilization of wealth and resources.

(The Universal House of Justice, from a message dated 1 March 2017 to the Bahá'ís of the World) [226]

Health

Let them also study whatever will nurture the health of the body and its physical soundness, and how to guard their children from disease.

('Abdu'l-Bahá, *Selections from the Writings of 'Abdu'l-Bahá*, no. 94.3) [227]

Make ye then a mighty effort, that the purity and sanctity which, above all else, are cherished by 'Abdu'l-Bahá, shall distinguish the people of Bahá; that in every kind of excellence the people of God shall surpass all other human beings; that both outwardly and inwardly they shall prove superior to the rest; that for purity, immaculacy, refinement, and the preservation of health, they shall be leaders in the vanguard of those who know. And that by their freedom from enslavement, their knowledge, their self-control, they shall be first among the pure, the free and the wise.

('Abdu'l-Bahá, *Selections from the Writings of 'Abdu'l-Bahá*, no. 129.14) [228]

O handmaiden of the Most High! Thy letter was received. Thou hast written that thou seekest to establish a new hospital and art arranging and planning it together with five other Bahá'í doctors. Should such a matter be accomplished, it would be most beneficial.

('Abdu'l-Bahá, from a Tablet—translated from the Persian) [229]

If the health and well-being of the body be expended in the path of the Kingdom, this is very acceptable and praiseworthy; and if it be expended to the benefit of the human world in general—even though it be to their material (or bodily) benefit—and be a means of doing good, that is also acceptable. But if the health and welfare of man be spent in sensual desires, in a life on the animal plane, and in devilish pursuits—then disease were better than such health; nay, death itself were preferable to such a life. If thou art desirous of health, wish thou health for serving the Kingdom. I hope that thou mayest attain perfect insight, inflexible resolution, complete health, and spiritual and physical strength in order that thou mayest drink from the fountain of eternal life and be assisted by the spirit of divine confirmation.

('Abdu'l-Bahá, cited in *Bahá'u'lláh and the New Era: An Introduction to the Bahá'í Faith* (Wilmette: Bahá'í Publishing, 2006), p. 127) [230]

Healing through purely spiritual forces is undoubtedly as inadequate as that which materialist physicians and thinkers vainly seek to obtain by resorting entirely to mechanical devices and methods. The best result can be obtained by combining the two processes: spiritual and physical.

(From a letter dated 12 March 1934 written on behalf of Shoghi Effendi to an individual believer) [231]

The enormous energy dissipated and wasted on war, whether economic or political, will be consecrated to such ends as will extend the range of human inventions and technical development, to the increase of the productivity of mankind, to the extermination of disease, to the extension of scientific research, to the raising of the standard of physical health, to the sharpening and refinement of the human brain, to the exploitation of the unused and unsuspected resources of the planet, to the prolongation of human life, and to the furtherance of any other agency that can stimulate the intellectual, the moral, and spiritual life of the entire human race.

(Shoghi Effendi, from a letter dated 11 March 1936, in *The World Order of Bahá'u'lláh*, p. 204)   [232]

You may be pleased to learn that information on AIDS is incorporated in many Bahá'í health education projects in Africa and throughout the world, emphasizing the importance of chastity, marital fidelity, the sacredness of marriage and the crucial importance of the family as the fundamental unit of society. Education about AIDS and human sexuality is likely to be most effective if it is conducted within the context of training focussed on the broader, spiritual and moral aspects of life, which would lead to the strengthening of families and communities.

(From a letter dated 15 November 2000 written on behalf of the Universal House of Justice to an individual believer)   [233]

Arts, Media, and Technology

It is permissible to study sciences and arts, but such sciences as are useful and would redound to the progress and advancement of the people. Thus hath it been decreed by Him Who is the Ordainer, the All-Wise.

(Bahá'u'lláh, *Tablets of Bahá'u'lláh Revealed after the Kitáb-i-Aqdas*, p. 26)   [234]

At the outset of every endeavour, it is incumbent to look to the end of it. Of all the arts and sciences, set the children to studying those which will result in advantage to man, will ensure his progress and elevate his rank.

(Bahá'u'lláh, *Tablets of Bahá'u'lláh Revealed after the Kitáb-i-Aqdas*, p. 168)   [235]

Erelong shall We bring into being through thee exponents of new and wondrous sciences, of potent and effective crafts, and shall make manifest through them that which the heart of none of Our servants hath yet conceived.

(Bahá'u'lláh, *The Summons of the Lord of Hosts: Tablets of Bahá'u'lláh* (Wilmette: Bahá'í Publishing, 2006), no. 1.67) [236]

"Arts, crafts and sciences uplift the world of being, and are conducive to its exaltation."

(Bahá'u'lláh, *Epistle to the Son of the Wolf,* p. 26) [237]

Blessed is he who in the days of God will engage in handicrafts. This is a bounty from God, for in this Most Great Dispensation it is acceptable in the sight of God for man to occupy himself in a trade which relieveth him of depending upon charity. The craft of every craftsman is regarded as worship.

(Bahá'u'lláh, from a Tablet—translated from the Persian) [238]

Whatever is written should not transgress the bounds of tact and wisdom, and in the words used there should lie hid the property of milk, so that the children of the world may be nurtured therewith, and attain maturity. We have said in the past that one word hath the influence of spring and causeth hearts to become fresh and verdant, while another is like unto blight which causeth the blossoms and flowers to wither. God grant that authors among the friends will write in such a way as would be acceptable to fair-minded souls, and not lead to cavilling by the people.

(Bahá'u'lláh, from a Tablet—translated from the Arabic and Persian) [239]

Would the extension of education, the development of useful arts and sciences, the promotion of industry and technology, be harmful things? For such endeavor lifts the individual within the mass and raises him out of the depths of ignorance to the highest reaches of knowledge and human excellence.

('Abdu'l-Bahá, *The Secret of Divine Civilization*, ¶25)   [240]

It is therefore urgent that beneficial articles and books be written, clearly and definitely establishing what the present-day requirements of the people are, and what will conduce to the happiness and advancement of society. These should be published and spread throughout the nation, so that at least the leaders among the people should become, to some degree, awakened, and arise to exert themselves along those lines which will lead to their abiding honor. The publication of high thoughts is the dynamic power in the arteries of life; it is the very soul of the world. Thoughts are a boundless sea, and the effects and varying conditions of existence are as the separate forms and individual limits of the waves; not until the sea boils up will the waves rise and scatter their pearls of knowledge on the shore of life.

('Abdu'l-Bahá, *The Secret of Divine Civilization*, ¶194)   [241]

Observe for instance that in other countries they persevered over a long period until finally they discovered the power of steam and by means of it were enabled easily to perform the heavy tasks which were once beyond human strength. How many centuries it would take if we were to abandon the use of this power and instead strain every nerve to invent a substitute. It is therefore preferable to keep on with the use of steam and at the same time continuously to examine into the possibility of there being a far greater force available. One should regard the other technological advances, sciences, arts and political formulae of proven usefulness in the same light—i.e., those procedures which, down the ages, have time and again been put to the test and whose many uses and advantages have demonstrably resulted in the glory and greatness of the state, and the well-being and progress of the people. Should all these be abandoned, for no valid reason, and other methods of reform be attempted, by the time such reforms might eventuate, and their advantages might be put to proof, many years would go by, and many lives. Meanwhile, "we are still at the first bend in the road."

('Abdu'l-Bahá, *The Secret of Divine Civilization*, ¶201)   [242]

In this new and wondrous Age, the unshakable foundation is the teaching of sciences and arts. According to explicit Holy Texts, every child must be taught crafts and arts, to the degree that is needful. Wherefore, in every city and village, schools must be established and every child in that city or village is to engage in study to the necessary degree.

('Abdu'l-Bahá, *Selections from the Writings of 'Abdu'l-Bahá*, no. 109.1.)   [243]

The day will come when the Cause will spread like wildfire when its spirit and teachings will be presented on the stage or in art and literature as a whole. Art can better awaken such noble sentiments than cold rationalizing, especially among the mass of the people.

(From a letter dated 10 October 1932 written on behalf of Shoghi Effendi to an individual believer)   [244]

With regard to the . . . magazine, . . . he suggests that more emphasis be laid on the number and quality of articles, and that the latter be written not only on specific Bahá'í subjects, but should cover a wide range of material, whether social, religious or humanitarian. The science section is, no doubt, very important and has a special appeal to the young and the newcomers.

(From a letter dated 30 May 1935 written on behalf of Shoghi Effendi to an individual believer)   [245]

The unity of the human race, as envisaged by Bahá'u'lláh, implies the establishment of a world commonwealth in which all nations, races, creeds and classes are closely and permanently united, and in which the autonomy of its state members and the personal freedom and initiative of the individuals that compose them are definitely and completely safeguarded. . . . The press will, under such a system, while giving full scope to the expression of the diversified views and convictions of mankind, cease to be mischievously manipulated by vested interests, whether private or public, and will be liberated from the influence of contending governments and peoples.

(Shoghi Effendi, from a letter dated 11 March 1936, in *The World Order of Bahá'u'lláh*, pp. 203–4)   [246]

Imbued with this excellence and a corresponding humility, with tenacity and a loving servitude, today's youth must move towards the front ranks of the professions, trades, arts and crafts which are necessary to the further progress of humankind—this to ensure that the spirit of the Cause will cast its illumination on all these important areas of human endeavour. Moreover, while aiming at mastering the unifying concepts and swiftly advancing technologies of this era of communications, they can, indeed they must also guarantee the transmittal to the future of those skills which will preserve the marvelous, indispensable achievements of the past.

(The Universal House of Justice, from a message dated 8 May 1985 to the Bahá'í Youth of the World)   [247]

The scientific and technological advances occurring in this unusually blessed century portend a great surge forward in the social evolution of the planet, and indicate the means by which the practical problems of humanity may be solved. They provide, indeed, the very means for the administration of the complex life of a united world. Yet barriers persist. Doubts, misconceptions, prejudices, suspicions and narrow self-interest beset nations and peoples in their relations one to another.

(The Universal House of Justice, from a message dated October 1985 to the Peoples of the World)   [248]

It is useful to bear in mind that the Internet is a reflection of the world around us, and we find in its infinitude of pages the same competing forces of integration and disintegration that characterize the tumult in which humanity is caught up.

(From a letter dated 9 April 2008 written on behalf of the Universal House of Justice to an individual believer)   [249]

The capacity of the institutions and agencies of the Faith to build unity of thought in their communities, to maintain focus among the friends, to channel their energies in service to the Cause, and to promote systematic action depends, to an extent, on the degree to which the systems and instruments they employ are responsive to reality, that is, to the needs and demands of the local communities they serve and the society in which they operate.

In this connection, we are instructed to provide a word of warning: The use of technology will, of course, be imperative to the development of effective systems and instruments . . . ; yet it cannot be allowed to define needs and dictate action.

(From a letter dated 30 March 2011 written on behalf of the Universal House of Justice to a National Spiritual Assembly) [250]

There is no doubt that modern technologies can be valuable instruments in the great enterprise of building a prosperous world civilization. Surely, however, as an individual committed to rural development, you are aware of the potentially destructive forces unleashed by a naïve implementation of technology in the name of modernity and globalization. For example, the introduction of the agricultural practice of monoculture in rural areas, intended to increase efficiency and yield for small landowners, has in some instances actually cost them their land; even if there is, ultimately, merit in moving toward modern agricultural practices, one cannot be blind to the tremendous cost in human suffering that may occur, and which might be mitigated by a change in approach. The statement in the letter was a reference to these negative tendencies, and not a general condemnation of technological development and progress, which are upheld by the teachings of the Faith. . . .

Bahá'ís involved in projects for social and economic development recognize that there are both benefits and pitfalls involved with the use of technology. The key question is, therefore, not whether to use technology, but how to use it. Approaches to development centred on the donation of goods and services, so characteristic of well-intentioned traditional religious charity and the programs of the welfare state, are known to have debilitating effects. The initial allure of the promised technologies often proves ephemeral. It is to this phenomenon that the phrase "technologies deceptively packaged" refers. It is hoped that the friends in the development field will weigh the technical issues and social forces involved and bring to bear a profound understanding of both science and religion, so that they may contribute to a sound approach that avoids the extremes of blind faith in materialism and a romantic attachment to tradition.

(From a letter dated 30 December 2014 written on behalf of the Universal House of Justice to an individual believer)   [251]

As you know, technological advancement is integral to the emergence of a global civilization. Indeed, the Internet is a manifestation of a development anticipated by the Guardian when, in describing the characteristics of a unified humanity, he foresaw that a "mechanism of world inter-communication will be devised, embracing the whole planet, freed from national hindrances and restrictions, and functioning with marvellous swiftness and perfect regularity." Yet, learning to utilize the Internet in a manner conducive to material and spiritual progress is an immense challenge.

. . . However, given that the Internet allows for the instantaneous dissemination of content among growing multitudes, wisdom and self-discipline are required lest the significance or dignity of the Teachings become compromised by an unbecoming, inaccurate, or trivialized presentation. . . .

. . . For example, while it may be beneficial to reflect on the nature and form of the core activities, especially in the context of the experience of a cluster or region, certain problems arise in attempting to create a site that aims to speak to Bahá'ís worldwide about the subject. Such an approach could lead to the cultural norms and values of a particular population being promoted to a universal audience—a pattern all too prevalent in the world today. There is also the danger of exerting an unintended influence on the process of learning unfolding at the grassroots, where individuals, communities, and institutions are acting as protagonists of their own growth and development. The perspectives offered in the following extract from the message dated 12 December 2011 from the House of Justice to all National Spiritual Assemblies—although in the specific context of artistic endeavours and supplementary educational materials—are especially relevant to aspects of culture mentioned above:

Propelled by forces generated both within and outside the Baháʾí community, the peoples of the earth can be seen to be moving from divergent directions, closer and closer to one another, towards what will be a world civilization so stupendous in character that it would be futile for us to attempt to imagine it today. As this centripetal movement of populations accelerates across the globe, some elements in every culture, not in accord with the teachings of the Faith, will gradually fall away, while others will be reinforced. By the same token, new elements of culture will evolve over time as people hailing from every human group, inspired by the Revelation of Baháʾuʾlláh, give expression to patterns of thought and action engendered by His teachings, in part through artistic and literary works. . . . We long to see, for instance, the emergence of captivating songs from every part of the world, in every language, that will impress upon the consciousness of the young the profound concepts enshrined in the Baháʾí teachings. Yet such an efflorescence of creative thought will fail to materialize, should the friends fall, however inadvertently, into patterns prevalent in the world that give licence to those with financial resources to impose their cultural perspective on others, inundating them with materials and products aggressively promoted.

(From a letter dated 9 October 2015 written on behalf of the Universal House of Justice to a National Spiritual Assembly) [252]

One of the most significant developments that mark the unfoldment of the Divine Plan at this time has been the advancements at the level of culture that the Baháʾí community has experienced and to which the House of Justice has in several of its messages referred. These advancements deserve profound reflection. Every devoted believer will surely wish to guard and further foster them. Accordingly, the friends must pay heed to their manner of communication which can do so much to impact the community's culture. They must aim to raise consciousness without awakening the insistent self, to disseminate insight without cultivating a sense of celebrity, to address issues profoundly but not court controversy, to remain clear in expression but not descend to crassness prevalent in common discourse, and to avoid deliberately or unintentionally setting the agenda for the community or, in seeking the approval of society, recasting the community's endeavors in terms that can undermine those very endeavors.

(From a letter dated 4 April 2018 written on behalf of the Universal House of Justice to a National Spiritual Assembly) [253]